The Coupon Way
to
Lower Food Prices

The Coupon Way to Lower Food Prices

By CAROLE KRATZ & ALBERT LEE

wp

Workman Publishing Company
New York

All rights reserved.

© 1973 by Carole Kratz and Albert Lee.
This book may not be reproduced in whole
or in part, by mimeograph or any other
means, without permission in writing.

First printing September 1973.

Workman Publishing Company
231 East 51 Street
New York, New York 10022.

Printed in the United States of America.

ISBN: 0-911104-28-3.

Contents

Introduction	7
Chapter One What's the Manufacturer's Gimmick?	12
Chapter Two Where Are All Those Offers?	24
Chapter Three Cashing in by Mail	50
Chapter Four Money Isn't Everything	61
Chapter Five Cash in Your Trash	79
Chapter Six You Gotta Get Organized	105
Chapter Seven Don't Shop It; Swap It	128
Chapter Eight Is There a Gambler in the House?	136
Chapter Nine Charity, Sweet Charity	141

Chapter Ten
Free for All 144

Chapter Eleven
The Graduation Lecture.......... 150

Glossary....................... 156

Introduction

Labels are money, and if you are the average American consumer with a predilection for getting the greatest value for every shopping dollar, then label and box-top refunding probably is not new to you. No doubt you have occasionally ripped an entry blank from a grocery store display to get a $1.00 refund on two boxes of detergent, saved cereal boxes or a few labels from cans of beans to send for a free kitchen clock or a child's toy, cut out newspaper ads to get $.25 off on a $.50 jar of peanut butter, or purchased a box of detergent with a free bath towel inside. In short, you already are an amateur refunder. What this book will do is introduce you to big-league refunding. We'll show you how to turn your trash into cash and worthwhile merchandise.

The average American family discards about $2.00 worth of labels *every day*. Most women are not aware that a refund is regularly offered on virtually every household product and packaged food, from ammonia to canned zucchini, by at least one manufacturer. General Mills, Green Giant, Lever Brothers, Procter & Gamble, General Foods, Pillsbury, Lipton, Borden, and all the other top producers con-

INTRODUCTION 8

tinuously offer thousands of refund opportunities. These have ranged from a $.06-off coupon to $25.00 for using Cheer for a year.

In addition to the cash offers, there are offers of free merchandise just for trying a manufacturer's products. These items range from cookie cutters to mink coats and Cadillacs. Thousands of American homes are filled with mixers, toasters, bowls, silverware, dishes, bathroom scales, baby furniture, and endless other items—all obtained free.

Advertising men estimate that manufacturers give away between $4.5 and $6 billion each year in cash refunds and free-merchandise offers, and the trend toward using such offers to stimulate sales is climbing each year. A survey by A.C. Nielsen Company (a refund clearinghouse) concluded that coupon distribution has jumped more than 65 per cent since 1965. According to a *Supermarket News* survey, nearly 70 per cent of all retailers feel that more offers will be made each year as consumers become increasingly economy-minded.

How many of those billions of dollars can you collect by becoming a dedicated refunder? That depends on how proficient you become. By knowing how refunding works, by subscribing to one of the more than fifty refunders' bulletins that list the offers, and by an elaborate system of swapping labels and offer blanks that you can't use for those that you can, you can earn as much as $200 a month in cash and merchandise. Your initial investment will consist of about a dollar for one or two sample copies of refund bulletins, some envelopes and postage stamps, and a few spare minutes each day. Your profits will begin in just a few weeks.

Any earnest refunder can save 50 per cent of her shopping bill, and even a modest effort will assure a 25 per cent saving. There is no excuse for any consumer, *with very little effort,* not to save 10 to 15 per cent. Just how much you will save depends partially upon how much you are now spending. At 1972 prices, an average American family of four spends about $3,400 a year on food and household supplies and can save as much as $1,700 a year through refunds. The larger the family, the larger the appetite and the more you save by refunding. Yet even this formula is not always an indication of refunding profits. There are many ingenious ways of obtaining more labels than you actually buy and, therefore, of receiving more profits. Many refunders profit handsomely by using labels and box tops discarded by housewives who don't make the effort to collect the rewards for themselves.

These profits, by their nature, are not taxable. This may not seem like much of a break at first glance, but remember that about 30 per cent of most people's earnings goes to city, county, state, and federal taxes. Thus, $1,000 of nontaxable income is equal to $1,300 of taxable income.

If you set your refunding profits aside (rather than mingling them with the family income), they soon add up. Many wives use their refunding money to buy Christmas presents or for personal needs. One New York woman saved her profits for eighteen months and used them to visit her family in England. A Montana grandmother uses her refunding to supplement her meager social security checks. No matter what you use it for, the money will come in handy, and you will have the satisfaction of knowing that you earned it.

But refunding will bring you more than dollars and cents. There are intangible pleasures and benefits of refunding. Active refunders are a special lot. They regularly correspond with one another to swap labels, order blanks, or trading stamps; and with all that letter writing, it's inevitable that many new friendships develop. The typical refunder has pen pals from coast to coast and soon becomes a part of the refunders' circle in her own neighborhood. Mainly because of this, most advocates speak of refunding as a profitable hobby rather than just a basement enterprise.

One San Diego woman even calls refunding "therapeutic." It gives her—and thousands of other women—the satisfaction of contributing to the family income.

But before you start flipping your box tops, you must ask yourself if *you* really are a potential refunder. Admittedly, it is stereotyping, but there is a certain kind of woman or man who becomes a successful refunder. Nearly all the scores of people we interviewed and corresponded with about this unique business had three things in common, characteristics that might well be considered the prerequisites for being a refunder.

First, you must be an adventurous eater. Because offers are constantly changing, you must be willing to switch brands every month. If you have a love affair going with a specific brand and wouldn't trade your preference for twice as much of another, than you can't be a very successful refunder. Refunds are offered on a wide range of products, so if there are finicky eaters in your family, refunding will be less profitable for you. Avid refunders consider this constant change of menu one of the most exciting aspects of refunding. In fact, many buy the refundable products *first* and then plan their menus around the free items already on hand. Because these products must appeal to large numbers of people, none are exotic. Furthermore, all are high-quality national brands. But there is enough variation to make housewives with rigid shopping habits nervous.

Second, you must get organized. You will have to keep track of hundreds of different offers, labels, and entry blanks. And you will have to plan your meals around those foods that offer refunds. Once you have learned a few tricks, this organization is not difficult.

Third, you must have refunding know-how. That is what this book is designed to supply.

CHAPTER ONE

What's the manufacturer's gimmick?

"You gotta have a gimmick" is the golden rule of promotion. Yul Brynner cut off his hair; rock musicians let theirs grow; Cracker Jack put a prize in every box; Grauman's Chinese Theatre had celebrities romping around in wet cement—all successful promotion gimmicks. Even presidential candidates and other politicians rely on gimmicks to sell themselves. The point is that gimmicks are respectable members of our social structure, and although it would be better for companies, celebrities, and especially politicians to stand on their merits, it isn't realistic to expect it.

The food and household industries are no exceptions. With federal regulation of food preparation and packaging, there is exceedingly little difference between national brands of corn or frozen potpies. There are nearly a hundred different soaps and detergents, all with pretty much the same ingredients. The patent-medicine people will candidly admit, if you press them, that one brand of aspirin is essentially the same as the next. Obviously, manufacturers cannot depend only on the merits of their products. In order to survive, they must rely on sales gimmickery: sing-song commercials, psychologically significant packages, and those ever-popular refund offers.

There are times when promotional offers are used to meet special needs. Because refund offers can be limited to a specific location, market researchers have found them more effective for spot advertising than mass communications. So when sales in one region fall below those in the rest of the company's sales district, refund offers are used to bolster the region.

Refunds often are aimed at altering the basic eating and living habits of American families, such as attempting to sell the convenience of prepared meat dishes in preference to do-it-yourself meals. Since you generally pay more for the convenience item, the refund is offered as an incentive to buy. (Right now the cheapest "meat" *is* prepared meat entrees! Banquet 2-lb. Salisbury Steak has been $1.29, though hamburger has gone from $.49 to $1.19 a pound.)

Refund offers also get a new product into stores. Between 20,000 and 30,000 new products are introduced each year, which is more than any supermarket has room for. Obviously, in order to get shelf space, a new product has to become enough of a household name for shoppers to ask for it and store managers to be assured it will sell. In a recent *Woman's Day* magazine survey, store managers indicated that the real value of couponing was that it allowed them to keep a more accurate supply of couponed items which they knew would sell. The refund offer meets this need by giving consumers a monetary reason for asking for the product and at the same time familiarizing the public (even people who would never refund) with the name.

Finally, when manufacturers switch the ingredients in their products or merely dress them up with a bright new package, refunds are used to introduce the change to the public. A change in name, package, or ingredients often does the trick in buoying up sales. The classic example is a fish called horse mackerel. No one would buy it because of its less-than-appetizing name. The name was changed to tuna fish, and with that well-advertised superficial shift came national popularity.

To many of us impressed by the technological age, this shotgun approach to advertising may seem rather archaic. Actually, it's one of the few methods that work.

The point of all this is that the manufacturers are growing fat by giving away their products through various types of promotional offers. The exposure gained spurs sales, which more than compensates for the giveaways. Your refunding will hurt no one; in fact, you will redeem your cash and merchandise refunds with the manufacturers' blessings.

The grocery store operator often complains about handling cents-off coupons and trading stamps and cluttering up his displays with refund-offer blanks, but he, too, stands to gain from the process. Refunds help to sell slow-moving items and encourage many women to visit the store frequently. Many refunders find they're buying more and better foods and still making a net profit.

Because refunds are get-acquainted offers, the manufacturer rarely tries to put one over on the public. But should he try, there are several agencies tailored to fitting him with a lawsuit. Most refund offers cross state lines and therefore qualify for jurisdiction by the Federal Trade Commission (FTC). Most refund offers are mailed; therefore the post-office inspector's department also regulates them. There are special federal regulatory agencies, such as the President's special assistant for consumer affairs, that investigate advertising practices; and thirty-nine states now have consumer-protection divisions, normally as part of the state attorney general's office. These agencies are concerned primarily with consumer fraud and can apply real pressure to a manufacturer on behalf of an outraged consumer.

For example, in 1971, Wilkinson offered

a special deal in which if you bought one of their razors they would either give you a second razor free or a $2.00 cash refund. The offer was made on a special package of Wilkinson razors. Alas, many people bought the razor and opened the box to get their coupon only to find out that the refund had expired.

Such shenanigans were clearly in violation of FTC regulations, and the agency jumped on Wilkinson with both feet, demanding compensation for the consumer. The company claimed that the entire mess was an inadvertent error and, with FTC encouragement, did everything in their power to rectify it. They sent a task force of two hundred to visit retailers and explain that the old expiration date was to be extended for another year. They placed ads in magazines explaining the mistake and offered to give the refund for expired coupons—or no coupon at all if an individual said he'd already tossed it out.

Wilkinson's reaction demonstrates a very significant point: The refunder herself has more coercive power than any regulatory agency over any company. She can refuse to buy a brand and tell her friends about the manufacturer's misconduct. The manufacturer fears consumer boycotting, so if his transgression is brought to his attention (as in the Wilkinson case), he will do everything in his power to re-establish good will. A refunder who feels that a merchandise offer was not of any real value or who has not received her cash refund from a company has only to write a polite letter to the manufacturer's public relations or customer relations department, pointing out the error without making sweeping accusations and innuendos of fraud. This technique gets the desired results.

The complaint letter should be sent to the address on the product package. The address on refund-offer forms typically belongs to a clearinghouse (such as the Nielsen Company of Clinton, Iowa) that processes refund offers for the company but is not directly connected with it. These clearinghouses do not have time to answer complaint letters and seldom forward them to manufacturers because, more often than not, the complaint deals with the way the refund offer was processed.

Whether you are writing a letter of complaint or simply asking for a cash refund, never identify yourself as a professional refunder. Most refunders we interviewed considered this a misnomer. They felt it applies in a positive way to bulletin editors and others who offer refunding services, and in a negative way to the few refunders who obtain quantities of labels and box tops at little or no cost and, without buying products, make collecting refunds virtually their entire livelihood. Obviously, the majority of even the most dedicated refunders are spending their money on the refund products before collecting the rewards, and cannot be considered "professionals" in any sense of the word.

From the companies' viewpoint, however, the term applies even to the buying avid refunder who switches brands without hesitation or trades her cat food labels for a neighbor's dog food labels. Many companies believe that this type of refunding does not serve the purpose of refund offers, which is to introduce a product to a consumer and, hopefully, to get the consumer to become a lifelong customer. The most dedicated refunders are bargain hunters *(cream skimmers, cherry pickers,* and *bargain babes,* as admen call them); they're not likely to stick with a brand after its refund offer has expired. They are pragmatists, not loyalists.

So in writing to a manufacturer, simply identify yourself as what you are: a consumer trying to get the greatest value for your dollar. Manufacturers will be anxious to do business with you. After all, it's to their advantage.

KINDS OF OFFERS

Many different kinds of offers are made. Some manufacturers tend to stick with only one form of refund or merchandise offer, but most vary their offerings. The sharp refunder should know enough about each kind of offer to take full advantage of it. The Carnation evaporated milk people, for example, usually make gift-incentive offers but occasionally promote a cash refund, such as their last offer, which gave $1.00 on a $.99 product.

Here are descriptions of the six basic kinds of promotional offers that you need to know about.

1. A refund offer gives cash, coupon, or merchandise entirely free for box tops or labels. From the consumer's viewpoint, the most important type of refund offer is the *cash refund*. Essentially, a company offers you cash for using one of its products. You buy the product, send in the required box tops or labels, and wait for the mailman to bring your refund ($.25, $.50, $1.00, or even $5.00) by return mail. Because the cash refund seems the most lucrative, some refunders won't bother with anything else. However, these cash-and-carry refunders are making a mistake; the other forms of offers supplement cash refunds nicely. For example, refund offers that give you a coupon on your next purchase are well worth taking advantage of. These coupons, which refunders call *store coupons,* are usually for substantial amounts off the retail price or the next purchase entirely free. Many refunders find they almost never pay for such common items as margarine, canned vegetables, and endless cleaning supplies.

Likewise, refund offers of free merchandise will bring the consumer a literal houseful of top-quality items. For example, as disposable diapers have been introduced over the past few years, the companies have boosted sales and encouraged use of their product by offering virtually every item of baby furniture entirely free.

2. Promotional cash-off coupons are redemption slips good for $.05, $.10, $.15, or more off the purchase price of a product. Such cash-off coupons are distributed through newspaper and magazine ads and also by direct mailings to "occupant," "boxholder," or other randomly selected mailing lists. All you have to do is turn the coupon in to the grocery clerk when you buy the specified product.

These small offers would be more trouble than they are worth if it were not for the fact that the same companies that give you cash-off coupons also give you cash refunds. By combining the two, your profits will increase. For example, a package of brown-and-serve rolls sells for $.89. You buy them with a $.15 cash-off coupon and pay only $.74; then you send in the endseal for the $.50 refund the company is also offering. If you deduct the cost of an $.08 stamp, you have purchased an $.89 food product for just $.32—less than half its cost to other shoppers. A little elementary arithmetic can give you an idea of just how much you can save this way. If you save on just one such item at each meal, you would pocket over $600 a year.

3. Money-plus offers give you merchandise for labels plus money. Quite frankly, most experienced refunders do not pay very much attention to money-plus offers because they realize that at some time the same items will probably be given absolutely free on a refund offer.

Nevertheless, a money-plus offer often represents a very good saving over the average retail price of the item offered. If you really need the item, compare the required fee with the average retail price and decide whether the offer will be advantageous for you.

Great bargains are available this way. The company wants you to try its product, not to make a profit on selling silverware, cameras, toys, or whatever it is offering as an incentive. For this reason, the merchandise is usually offered at what it cost the company, and this price is exceedingly low because the company buys in boxcar quantities.

4. Point coupon offers are low-value, long-term collection programs. Betty Crocker, Raleigh cigarette, and Red Star coupons are notable examples. Point coupons are better suited to the collection efforts of charitable groups than they are to individual savings. Catalogs detailing the points needed for various items are always offered by the sponsoring companies, and the address is usually on each coupon. If saving them for yourself doesn't seem to be worth the bother, save your point coupons anyway and donate them to a charity.

5. Trading stamps are a bonus given by a retailer as a reward for patronizing his store. In some states, trading stamps must be given a cash-redemption value, but they are worth more if redeemed in the traditional way for any of the thousands of items listed in the brand's trading-stamp catalog or displayed in their local redemption stores. There are more than two hundred different brands of trading stamps, but the biggest companies are S&H Green, Top Value, Blue Chip, Gold Bond, and Plaid.

6. Sweepstakes and contests are not actually refunds in the sense that you can be assured of a return on your efforts, but they can, nonetheless, be money-making ventures. (Chapter Eight is devoted to this subject.) The primary difference between sweepstakes and contests is the skill needed to win. In a contest, you are competing for a prize by submitting a jingle or a slogan. In a sweepstake, prizes are awarded simply on the basis of a drawing. In both cases, the only entry fee is a box top or label from the sponsor's product.

Although the promotional rewards offered in each category represent a real value savings, many factors must be considered in evaluating their true worth. You may pay more to shop at a store giving trading stamps, but if you must shop there anyway, the savings are worthwhile. Merchandise is of value only if you can put the item to use; experienced refunders know that a stockpile of free items comes in handy for all kinds of gift-giving needs. Point coupons will add up over the years, but many housewives just don't have the time to fuss with the clipping, counting, and saving; yet they can enjoy the satisfaction of tearing the coupons off and periodically sending them to a collecting charity. The Bethesda Lutheran Home for Retarded Children, for example, gets a great portion of its operating funds through donations of point coupons and trading stamps. Companies sponsoring both point-coupon and trading-stamp programs will purchase any item for a group (such as school buses and playground equipment).

In fact, all six kinds of offers can be extremely rewarding if used correctly. But if only one method had to be utilized exclusively, the choice of most refunders would doubtlessly be refund offers. They are the most lucrative and the easiest to collect on and will, therefore, receive the most of our attention in this book.

Like any special field, refunding has a language all its own. We have provided a Glossary (which you will find at the back of the book) to help you understand refunders' terms.

CHAPTER TWO

Where are all those offers?

You probably were not aware that most grocery stores carry baby clothing and infant accessories until you had a baby or that stores have whole counters devoted to dog supplies until you bought a dog. Well, you will find that the same thing is true once you become interested in refunding. You will be amazed by all the refund offers around you. The typical consumer is, in fact, constantly being bombarded with refund offers by every form of communication media.

NEWSPAPERS AND MAGAZINES

Daily newspapers carry many refund offers and cash-off coupons in the grocery store advertisements and in direct manufacturer product ads. Traditionally, the heaviest days for such advertising are Wednesday and Thursday, the pre-weekend shopping days. Sunday papers, especially in large cities, also carry cash-off coupons and refund offers. If you don't subscribe to your local newspaper, you'll want to borrow yesterday's issue from a neighbor and scan it for refund offers.

Magazine advertisements often contain refund offers and cash-off coupons. This is especially true of women's magazines and family-interest publications. The smart refunder thumbs through every magazine she comes across.

Because the coupons in magazines are as good as cash, you may want to obtain copies of the publication in quantity. There are several ways to do this fairly cheaply. You can buy copies at a discount from several companies who specialize in this kind of service.* You will probably pay even less if you can find a local magazine wholesaler and buy his returns in quantity. The wholesaler gets rebates from the magazine companies on all copies he doesn't sell. But because the magazine companies only ask that he return the magazine covers (not the entire magazines), he has thousands of month-old magazines to get rid of. Typically, he donates some copies to in-

---

*One of the best is Publishers Clearing House, Department E., 382 Main Street, Port Washington, New York 11050.

stitutions and sells the rest for scrap paper. If you offer him a little more than the going salvage rate, you'll get all you need.

A month seldom goes by without neighborhood kids collecting for a paper drive, which means you have another ready source of newspaper coupons. Offer the youngster or the sponsoring organization a fee for allowing you to go through the stacks of papers with a pair of scissors. You'll get many more coupons than you can use. (In Chapter Seven, we'll tell you how to trade these in for coupons and refund forms you can use.)

SUPERMARKETS

Pads of refund-offer blanks are usually posted on supermarket displays. These offer blanks are snapped up quickly, so if the display card is there but the forms are gone, ask your grocer for more. The cardboard backing often tells you where you can write for an offer blank or simply gives you instructions on how to cash in on the offer without a form. The conscientious refunder makes the rounds of all stores in her area because some stores carry different brands and therefore have different refund-offer blanks on display.

Frequently, refund offers are printed on special packages of the product itself, or the offer coupons are inside the package, so you will have to buy the product in order to get all the necessary details of the offer.

Inspect such packages closely for an expiration date so that you don't buy a container with an expired offer enclosed. Food and Drug Administration (FDA) rules require the date and pertinent information to be on the outside of the package.

OTHER REFUNDERS

Fellow refunders are another good source of information. Once you get involved with refunding, you will meet neighbors with whom you can exchange refund news.

OTHER SOURCES

Supermarket News, a weekly paper for storekeepers, contains information on promotional offers before the news is released to the general public.* This is a fine source of valuable and accurate information about the retailing industry as a whole.

What is commonly called *junk mail* is yet another source of refund offers. These cash-off and merchandise offers are sent out from the sponsoring company or from a direct-mailing business. Once you send in some cash-refund offers, you mysteriously end up on everyone's mailing lists.

---

*A one-year subscription costs $3.00 and is available from *Supermarket News,* 7 East 12th Street, New York, New York 10003.

So read your junk mail before chucking it into the garbage.

Advertisers are busily looking for new and ingenious ways to get refund offers into your hands. One innovative approach uses a coupon-dispensing machine (patented by Tel-A-Dex Corporation of Massachusetts) in grocery stores, which gives out coupons one at a time. In a survey at Roche Brothers Supermarkets, a small Eastern chain, the Tel-A-Dex machine coupons had a 78.7 per cent redemption rate, compared with a 3 to 15 per cent redemption rate for newspaper and magazine coupons.

BULLETINS

All these sources are excellent, but the best source of refunding information, the one used most frequently by successful refunders, is the refund bulletin. There are between forty and fifty-five refund bulletins being printed or mimeographed and distributed in the United States. The bulletins publish most of the national offers (as many as 1,000 current offers) and are mailed to refunders all over the country. Most of the bulletins are printed by housewife-refunders and are not, as a whole, professionally produced; but the information is there in abundance, and that makes the bulletins a refunder's must.

Some bulletins list cash-refund offers

only; others include merchandise offers as well. Some contain ads for an endless variety of form and label exchanges; others don't. Some even include recipes for planning meals using only refund foods. Some are delivered by third-class mail; some, by first class. Some are printed weekly; some, monthly; some, quarterly. Many are issued ten times a year, skipping the slow refund months of July and December.

Bulletins also vary in accuracy. The companies that make refund offers do not supply information to the bulletin publishers. Because these basement editors must receive their information on offers secondhand, some bulletins botch the fact gathering and report obsolete offers or are unaware that the expiration date or other important data have been omitted.

Most of the inaccuracies in refund bulletins can be directly attributed to the companies doing the advertising. According to Niles Eggleston, who produced the first refund bulletin a score of years ago, "The manufacturers simply will not write all the rules on the order forms or into their ads." Eggleston has made many attempts to cooperate with the companies in improving the accuracy of available information, but he got no takers.

There are, however, some exceptionally accurate bulletins that have years of reporting experience behind them. If you choose a good bulletin, most of the scurrying around in search of refund information can be eliminated. In effect, a good editor does most of the work for thousands of subscribers.

How to Choose a Bulletin

Which bulletins should you subscribe to? That's a question only you can answer. If you like recipes and poetry, then you'll want a generalized refund bulletin that includes these nonessentials. If you favor a no-nonsense approach, you should stick with the straight refund-listing bulletins. As a beginner, you should first purchase a catch-up bulletin that lists all long-term and undated offers. Most bulletins do not print the same offers month after month, so the catch-up bulletin is the only way for a beginner to know what she's been missing. *Golden Opportunities* and *Money Tree* are two such bulletins (see the list of bulletins at the end of this chapter).

Most refunders subscribe to more than one bulletin or trade bulletins with other refunders. In this way you won't miss offers that any single bulletin could easily overlook. Remember, third-class mail is slow, so it is a good idea to subscribe to at least one bulletin that is mailed first class. Generally, these bulletins do not have as many extra features (their weight must be kept down), but they are far more current than the fatter bulletins mailed under bulk rates. At least one of the bulletins you subscribe to should contain a good classified ad section that lists form and label trades. The more you become involved in refunding, the more you will need such trading opportunities.

The way a bulletin is organized should be a significant factor in your choice. Many bulletins merely throw all offers in as they arrive, and you must hunt and pick. Others number the offers so that you can have a reference point, and some bulletins list them in alphabetical order or group them by expiration dates. Experienced refunders are almost equally divided in preferring bulletins listing offers alphabetically or by expiration dates, and many refunders subscribe to both types to take advantage of the best features of each.

Most bulletins sell sample copies, and it is prudent to buy several different samples before deciding on any one bulletin.

Here is a list of most of the refund bulletins currently being published. We have tried to weed out all those with a reputation for questionable reporting. Furthermore, some bulletin editors objected to being cited in a widely circulated book for fear they would receive more business than they could handle; thus, the list does not include these dissenters. We have tried to give as much information as possible to help readers choose worthy sample bulletins.

CALIFORNIA SWAP N SAVE, 2305 West Cornell, Fresno, California 93705. Editor, Nadean Ferolito; sample, $.50; year, $3.50; classified ads, $.03 per word.

Published monthly since 1971, *California Swap N Save* is a neat bulletin with a good presentation of refund information. The offers are organized according to month of expiration. The April, 1973, issue listed about 135 refund offers. This bulletin is mimeographed and mailed first class. Circulation is under 1,000.

DEL'S DOUGH BACK, Box 171, Lyons, Illinois 60534. Editor, Del Novak; sample, $.50.

In this monthly bulletin, offers are organized by month of expiration. About 45 offers were listed in its November, 1972, issue.

EASY MONEY REFUND BULLETIN, P.O. Box 1012, Jackson, Michigan 49204. Editor, A. Comperchio; sample, $.50; year, $5.00; classified ads, $.02 per word.

Easy Money has been issued monthly since 1969. There were 85 offers listed in the January, 1972, issue. This duplicator-printed bulletin is mailed first class. Circulation is under 1,000.

FASTBUCK REFUND PAPER, Prairie Mountain Route, Llano, Texas 78643. Editor, Evelyn Wade; sample, no price given.

This monthly bulletin listed about 60 offers in the October, 1972, issue. Because no sample price is given, we suggest you send a SASE to the editor for further information.*

---

*SASE means the sender provides a self-addressed, stamped envelope.

FINDERS KEEPERS, Route 2, Box 36, Kinsman, Ohio 44428. Editor, Fran Verina; sample, $.50; year, $3.50; classified ads, $.05 per word.

Finders Keepers, published monthly since 1970 or 1971, presents offer information clearly. Offers are separated into two sections: those that may not require a form and those that do. This division makes locating specific brand information somewhat difficult. The April, 1973, issue had about 110 refund offers. This bulletin is neatly mimeographed and is mailed third class. Circulation is under 1,000.

FIRE FLY REPORTER, Box 95, Westbrook, Minnesota 56183. Editor, Isabelle Scarset; sample, $.70; year, $5.00; classified ads, $.06 per word.

Fire Fly has been printed monthly since 1966. The offers are not organized to aid the reader in locating information, but there is an alphabetical index. The May, 1973, issue featured about 180 offers. Printed as a mini-newspaper, this bulletin is mailed first class. Exact subscription figures are not available but the editor claims 10,000 readers.

FUNDS WITH REFUNDS, P.O. Box 52, Washington, Indiana 47501. Editor, Mildred Green; sample, $.50; year, $4.50; classified ads, $.04 per word.

Funds with Refunds has been published monthly since 1968, but Mildred Green has been its editor for just a few months. Offers are organized in sections by month of expiration. There were about 90 refund offers in the May, 1973, issue. This bulletin is mimeographed and mailed first class. Because the editor has just taken over a small subscribership, circulation figures are not yet available for publication.

GOLD'N REFUNDS, Box 262, Hannibal, Ohio 43931. Editor, Carole Kratz; sample, $.60; year, $5.00; classified ads, $.15 per word, swap ads, $.05 per word to subscribers.

This monthly bulletin, originally called *Refund Reports*, has been known for soundly researched reporting since 1966. It has been edited by Carole Kratz for over two years. Offers are listed alphabetically and there is an expiration-month recap list for the reader's convenience. There were 231 new refund offers listed in the June, 1973, issue. Printed by offset, this twelve-to-sixteen page booklet is mailed first class. Circulation is under 10,000.

THE GRAPEVINE, 6016 West Grace, Chicago, Illinois 60634. Editor, Karen Madej; sample, $.55; year, $4.00; classified ads, $.03 per word.

Karen Madej has been publishing *The Grapevine* since 1969. Offers are arranged alphabetically. The June, 1973, issue listed about 125 offers. This mimeographed monthly bulletin is mailed first class. Circulation is under 1,000.

GREEN BACK REFUNDS, Rose Hill Road, Wales, Tennessee 38484. Editor, unknown; sample, $.40.

This monthly bulletin lists offers by month of expiration. About 70 offers were presented in its June, 1971, issue.

HERTHA FEROLITO'S REFUNDER, 1521 East Vassar, Fresno, California 93704. Editor, Hertha Ferolito; sample, $.50; year, $3.50; classified ads, $.04 per word.

Hertha Ferolito, former co-editor of *California Swap N Save,* took over this bulletin in 1972. A neat and well-organized bulletin, published monthly since 1963, it presents offers in easy-to-locate alphabetical order. There were about 125 refund offers in the May, 1973, issue. The bulletin is mimeographed and mailed first class. Circulation is under 2,000.

THE HOUSEWIFE REPORTER, 14805 Laplaisance Road East, Monroe, Michigan 48161. Editor, Joyce Navarre; sample, $.50; year, $4.50; classified ads, $.03 per word.

Published monthly since 1970, *The Housewife Reporter* has to be considered one of the best monthly bulletins available. Although the offers are not organized to aid the reader in locating information, there is an index. What raises this bulletin far above others with similar amounts of information and format is its excellent printing, done professionally by computer. The bulletin is easy to read, and boldface type makes key wording stand out. The April, 1973, issue listed about 125 refund offers. It is mailed first class. Circulation is under 5,000.

THE INFORMER REFUND BULLETIN, P.O. Box 202, West Branch, Michigan 48661. Editor, R. C. Huston; sample, no price given; year, $4.50; classified ads, $.05 per word.

The Informer has been published monthly since 1969. Offers are grouped in about ten different sections by value and/or type. Information is difficult to locate. The May, 1973, issue listed about 110 offers. Mailed first class, this bulletin is mimeographed. Its circulation is under 2,000.

JAYBEE'S, Box 39, Valley Park, Missouri 63088. Editor, Claudine Moffatt; sample, $.50; year, $4.00; classified ads, $.05 per word.

Jaybee's, a hobby and contest magazine with a refunding section, has been published monthly since 1962. There is no index of offers to aid locating information quickly. The May, 1973, issue listed about 180 offers. This offset-printed booklet is mailed second class. Circulation is about 5,000.

KRAFTY HOBBY CRAFTS, P.O. Box 2122, Hyattsville, Maryland 20784. Editor, Daisy Austin; sample, $.40; year, $4.00; classified ads, $.05 per word.

Krafty Hobby Crafts is primarily a craft and hobby magazine, but it includes a small refund-information section. Published since 1969, it is currently issued bimonthly (six issues per year). The January-February, 1973, issue listed about 40 refund offers. Printed booklets are mailed second class.

M&M REFUND NEWS, 90 Extension Street, Mansfield, Pennsylvania 16933. Editor, Lorene Moore; sample, $.50; year, $4.00.

Lorene Moore recently took over editorship of this bulletin, which has been published monthly for about three years. The May, 1973, issue featured about 30 offers, not organized. This mimeographed bulletin is mailed first class. Its circulation is under 1,000.

MO-KAN REPORTER, Box 352, Shawnee Mission, Kansas 66201. Editor, Matt Thomas; sample, $.50; year, $4.00; classified ads, $.02 per word.

Mo-Kan Reporter has been published monthly since 1970. Offers are grouped according to month of expiration. The May, 1973, issue listed about 95 offers. This mimeographed bulletin is mailed first class and has a circulation of under 1,000.

MONEY BACK, Route 1, Box 125, Grand Junction, Michigan 49065. Editor, Izola Meyers; sample, $.50; year, $3.75; classified ads, $.04 per word.

Money Back has been published each month since 1970. Offers are organized by expiration month, but an alphabetical index will save readers a great deal of time locating the offers in the different sections. The April, 1973, issue contained about 120 refund offers. This mimeographed booklet-bulletin is mailed first class. Its circulation is under 1,000.

THE MONEY MAKER BULLETIN, P.O. Box 13564, St. Louis, Missouri 63138. Editor, Carol Backs; sample, $.50; year, $4.00; classified ads, $.03 per word.

This dependable monthly bulletin has been published since 1969. The offers are not organized, but there is an alphabetical index to assist you in finding information. The May, 1973, issue contained about 125 refund offers. Printed as a mini-newspaper, this bulletin is mailed first class and has a circulation of under 3,000.

NO MONEY ACCEPTED REFUND PAPER, Box 806, Malibu, California 90265. Editor, Kitty Houghtaling.

As the name implies, this monthly paper is not sold. It is traded for items of value to refunders, such as labels, and is more of a swap paper than a refund bulletin. However, the August, 1972, issue listed about 55 offers. Send SASE to the editor if you want more information.

PANTRY PAY-OFFS, P.O. Box 2525, Livonia, Michigan 48150. Editors, Marian Moore and Lucy Young; sample, $.35; year, $3.50; classified ads, $.03 per word.

Pantry Pay-Offs is a very concise mini-bulletin that has been published monthly since 1971. The offers are in alphabetical order in the main section, with subdivisions for gift offers, nondated offers, and last-minute additions, and locating information is a bit difficult. The May, 1973, issue contained about 90 refund offers. A clearly printed leaflet, it is mailed first class. The editors decline to make any circulation figures public.

PIGGY BANK REFUND NEWS, P.O. Box 6, Greendale, Wisconsin 53129. Editor, unknown; sample, no price given.

The March, 1971, issue of this neatly presented monthly bulletin listed about 80 offers alphabetically. No sample copy price was given, so you may wish to send an SASE and ask for further and current information.

THE QUARTER BACK, Route 1, Box 4, Johnson Creek, Wisconsin 53038. Editor, Jody Hinstorff; sample, $.50; year, $3.50; classified ads, $.04 per word.

Jody Hinstorff has published this monthly bulletin for two years. (It was established by another editor about five years ago.) Offers are organized by month of expiration. A sample copy (April, 1973) listed 95 refund offers. This mimeographed bulletin is mailed first class. Circulation is well under 1,000.

QUICK SILVER, Milford, New York 13807. Editor, Niles Eggleston; sample, $.50; year, $4.00.

Quick Silver claims to be the first refund bulletin and has been published monthly since August, 1954. The listings are not alphabetical or organized for the convenience of readers. The April, 1973, issue presented 66 refund offers. There is no advertising section. *Quick Silver* is mimeographed and is mailed first class. Circulation is about 5,000.

THE QUIET MOUSE, 1722 Cheryl Street, Billings, Montana 59101. Editor, Janice Love; sample, $.60.

The Quiet Mouse lists offers by month of expiration. The February, 1972, issue contained about 45 refund offers.

THE REFUNDER, Box 888, Manhattan Beach, California 90266. Editor, Sonja Winter; sample, $.50; year, $5.00; classified ads, for members only.

This interesting bulletin has been published monthly since 1968. Refund offers are listed in sections by their month of expiration, and the inexperienced reader might find the intricate format, which uses abbreviations, confusing. However, the information is accurate and reliable. The April, 1973, issue listed about 110 offers. This printed bulletin is mailed first class. Circulation is estimated at about 1,000.

THE REFUNDER, Box 373, Northwood, North Dakota 58267. Editor, Lilly Froslie; sample, $.40; classified ads, $.02 per word.

The June, 1971, issue of this neat little bulletin listed about 50 offers alphabetically.

THE REFUNDERS GAZETTE REFUND MAGAZINE, 128 Barton Street, Buffalo, New York 14213. Editor, Vivian Jean

Lafalce; sample, $.50; year, $4.50; classified ads, $.02 per word.

This bulletin has been published monthly since 1970. The paper is neat, and the information is clearly presented, with offers organized according to month of expiration. A sample copy (February, 1973) listed 64 refund offers. The paper is duplicated and is mailed first class. Circulation is well under 1,000.

REFUNDER'S WHITE PAPER, Leitchfield, Kentucky 42754. Editor, Lillian White; sample, $.60; year, $5.00; classified ads, $.04 per word.

This informative bulletin began monthly publication in 1968. Offers are divided into sections according to month of expiration. About 130 refund offers were listed in the April, 1973, issue. This bulletin is mimeographed and mailed first class. Circulation is under 1,000.

REFUND-O-RAMA, P.O. Box 5773, Detroit, Michigan 48239. Editor, R. O. Rama; sample, $.50; year, $4.50; classified ads, $.05 per word.

A compact mini-bulletin, *Refund-O-Rama* has been issued on a monthly basis since 1970. Offers are listed in alphabetical order, thus making the reader's job easier. The April, 1973, issue contained about 90 refund offers. This clearly printed leaflet is mailed first class and has a circulation of 1,500.

REFUND ROUND-UP, 548 W. Graisbury Avenue, Audubon, New Jersey 08106. Editor, Doris McClelland; sample, $.50; year, $4.00.

Refund Round-up has been a monthly refunding regular since 1964. All past editors have maintained top reporting standards, and Doris McClelland has, in her two years of editorship, done a fine job. Offers are organized in sections by expiration month, with an alphabetical index to assist you in locating information. There were about 110 refund offers listed in the April, 1973, issue. There is no advertising section. A neatly printed folder, mailed first class, *Refund Round-up* has a circulation of under 3,000.

REFUND WORLD, Box 16001, Philadelphia, Pennsylvania 19114. Editor, P. J. Keating; sample, $.45.

The November, 1972, issue of *Refund World* contained about 75 offers, not organized in any particular order.

SILVER LININGS, 1612 Ferry, Waukegan, Illinois 60085. Editor, Karen Quigley; sample, $.50; year, $4.00; classified ads, $.03 per word.

Silver Linings is a new monthly bulletin, but the editor has had previous experience in publishing refunding bulletins. The offers are not organized, but there is an alphabetical index to assist the reader in locating information. The April, 1973, issue contained about 100 refund offers. This almost pocket-sized booklet is neatly printed, and is mailed first class. The editor did not wish to estimate circulation because the bulletin has only been out for a few months.

SILVER-O-GRAMS, Box 686, Manchester, Missouri 63088. Editor, Claudine Moffatt; sample, $.25; classified ads, $.03 per word.

This monthly bulletin has been published for six years by Claudine Moffatt, who also publishes the monthly bulletins *Jaybee's* and *Money Tree*. Refund offers are organized in roughly alphabetical order. A sample copy (May, 1973) contained about 55 offers. This mimeographed bulletin is mailed by bulk rate and has a circulation of over 1,000.

THE TEXAS ROUND-UP, P.O. Box 307, Center, Texas 75935. Editor, Marie Doggett; sample, $.50; classified ads, $.02 per word.

Offers are clearly presented in alphabetical order. There were about 100 offers listed in a sample copy (March, 1971).

THAT'S MONEY HONEY, 6944 Bret Harte Drive, San Jose, California 95120. Editor, Marion Hilton; sample, $.50; year, $3.50; classified ads, $.02 per word.

That's Money Honey, first published two years ago, has been delivering monthly issues under Marion Hilton's editorship for the past year and a half. It is a well-organized bulletin, listing refund offers in alphabetical order. The May, 1973, issue contained about 120 offers. This bulletin is mimeographed, is mailed first class, and has a circulation of well under 1,000.

TOPS IN SWAPS—REFUND TREASURES, Box 4391 West Station, Meridian, Mississippi 39301. Editor, Lea James; sample, $.50; year, $4.00; classified ads, $.03 per word to subscribers, $.05 per word for others.

This bulletin has been published monthly since 1970. Offers are listed in sections by expiration month, and there is no index. The May, 1973, sample issue featured about 135 refund offers. This mimeographed bulletin is mailed first class and has a circulation of under 2,000.

TRADE WIND, Route 6, Box 73, Greenfield, Indiana 46140. Editor, LaVonne Patterson; sample, $.50; year, $4.00; classified ads, $.03 per word.

Trade Wind has been published monthly since 1970 and is one of the more chatty, gossipy refund bulletins. Listings are not organized for the reader's convenience, but there is an index. Abbreviations are used, which new readers may find confusing, but there's lots of information sandwiched in this paper. The April, 1973, issue contained about 150 refund offers. A printed bulletin, it is mailed first class. Circulation is under 3,000.

THE TREASURE CHEST, P.O. Box 1132, New Brunswick, New Jersey 08903. Editor, Jeanette Turniansky; sample, $.50; year, $4.50; classified ads, $.05 per word.

Since it was established in 1966, this bulletin passed through the hands of several editors before Jeanette Turniansky took it over in 1971. Just recently, *Refund News/Hobby Lobby,* a well-known major bulletin, merged with *Treasure Chest.* Refund offers are organized in sections by month of expiration; there is no index. The March, 1973, sample issue featured about 130 offers. This mimeographed bulletin is mailed first class and has a circulation of 4,500.

TREASURE HUNT, Box 426, Vandergrift, Pennsylvania 15690. Editor, Karen Stevenson; sample, $1.00; year, $4.75; classified ads, $.04 per word.

Treasure Hunt has been published bimonthly (six issues per year) since 1970. Offers are divided into several groups, and except for an alphabetical index, locating information might well be impossible. There were about 175 refund offers listed in the April-May, 1973, issue. *Treasure Hunt* is mailed, first class, and has a circulation of about 2,000.

WAGON-WHEEL-ROLLS, Route 1, Box 222, Crete, Nebraska 68333. Editor, G. J. Lauenroth; sample, $.50; year, $5.00.

This monthly bulletin has been regularly published since 1967. The information is accurate but not well organized for easy locating. The April, 1973, issue listed about 115 refund offers. This bulletin is mimeographed and is mailed first class. Circulation is under 1,000.

WINTERS SWAPPIN' SHOPPE, Box 705, Williamsburg, Indiana 47393. Editor, Jane Winters; sample, $.50; year, $4.00.

This bulletin is published monthly, and its primary content is swap offers on labels and so forth. The May, 1973, issue listed about 50 offers. This mimeographed bulletin is mailed first class and has a circulation of about 3,000.

YOUR REFUND NEWS REPORTER, P.O. Box 12, Buffalo, New York 14226. Editor, Marian Iannello; sample, $.50; year, $4.00; classified ads, $.03 per word.

This bulletin is noted for neat, reliable reporting and has been published monthly since 1971. Offers are presented alphabetically. The sample issue (May, 1973) contained about 135 refund offers. This mimeographed bulletin is mailed first class. Circulation is under 1,000.

Publishing a bulletin requires lots of work but very little capital investment, and it is not unusual for new bulletins to be published only to fold in a matter of weeks or months. Although we have seen past issues of the following bulletins, we have not been able to confirm their current publication status. If you want further information, you should write to the bulletin's editor. Be sure to send an SASE.

GLORIA PLESE, 5974 North 80th Street, Milwaukee, Wisconsin 53218.

THE GOLDEN EGG, 832 Dilger, Rapid City, South Dakota 57701.

BULLETINS

HAPPY CIRCLE NEWS, 212 Bruce Street, Scotia, New York 12302.

We have not been able to determine if this bulletin lists refund offers.

LINDA LEES ENTERPRISES, 210 Fifth Avenue, New York, New York 10010.

MAIL CALL, 1714 Brintnall, Brunswick, Ohio 44212.

THE MONEY BUCKET, 117½ W. Prospect, Ottawa, Illinois 61350.

MONEY TALK, 1714 Brintnall, Brunswick, Ohio 44212.

PUT MONEY IN THE BANK, Route 3, Box 260A, Bellefonte, Pennsylvania 16823.

REFUNDER'S GOLD, Route 1, Falls of Rough, Kentucky 40119.

REFUND NEWS, 2614 Weisman, Wheaton, Maryland 20902.

REFUND NEWS LETTER, Route 4, Oswego, New York 13126.

REFUND NEWS SERVICE LETTER, Box 448, Keddie, California 95952.

SHAKER NEWS, Route 5, Muscatine, Iowa 52761.

Past issues of this hobby magazine had a small section devoted to refund offers.

SWAPS & REFUNDS, 2039 Walnut, Ashland, Pennsylvania 17921.

WEEKLY PANTRY REFUNDS, 5425 Station Road, Blissfield, Michigan 49228. Editor, Ed Bailey; sample, $.15.

WHERE ARE ALL THOSE OFFERS?

The March, 1971, issue of this bulletin, which was then being published weekly, listed about 15 refund offers.

Recap Bulletins The following special bulletins are known among refunders as *recaps*. Essentially, they present offers that were made over the last several months and are believed to be still current.

GOLD DIGGERS, Route 2, Box 36, Kinsman, Ohio 44428. Editor, Fran Verina; copy, $2.00.

Gold Diggers has been issued twice a year since 1970 by the editor of *Finders Keepers*. It lists only dated offers, grouped into several sections. Locating information is quite difficult. The Spring, 1973, issue featured about 350 offers. This mimeographed booklet is mailed third class and has a circulation of under 1,000.

GOLDEN OPPORTUNITIES, Box 262, Hannibal, Ohio 43931. Editor, Carole Kratz; copy, $1.50; year, $5.50 (four copies); classified ads, $.05 per word.

Golden Opportunities features long-term dated or nondated offers and has been published quarterly since 1970 by the editor of *Gold'n Refunds*. Offers are listed in alphabetical order. The April-June, 1973, issue listed about 950 offers. Over 300 offers that don't require mail-in forms were spotlighted. Other features include a long freebie list and readers' letters. This forty-four-page booklet is printed by offset and is mailed first class. Circulation is under 6,000.

MONEY TREE, Box 638, Manchester, Missouri 63011. Editor, Claudine Moffatt; sample, $1.25; year, $12.50.

This monthly manual has been published by the editor of *Jaybee's* and *Silver-O-Grams* since 1967. The May, 1973, issue listed about 550 offers. This booklet is printed by offset and is mailed first class. Circulation is about 2,000.

REFUNDER'S DELIGHT, P.O. Box 547, Ferndale, Washington 98248. Editor, Dorothy Halldorson; sample, $.60; year, $5.00; classified ads, $.03 per word.

Published monthly since 1972, *Refunder's Delight* continues to list each offer until it expires. The May, 1973, issue featured about 200 offers arranged in alphabetical order. Printed by offset, this bulletin is mailed first class and has a circulation of about 3,000.

SUMMARY BULLETIN OF LONG TERM OFFERS, P.O. Box 12, Buffalo, New York 14226. Editor, Marian Iannello; sample, $1.50; year, $4.00 (three issues); classified ads, $.03 per word.

This bulletin has been published by the editor of *Your Refund News Reporter* since 1972. It is mimeographed and mailed first class. Circulation is under 1,000.

YEARBOOK, Route 6, Box 73, Greenfield, Indiana 46140. Editor, LaVonne Patterson; copy, $1.50.

This annual recap manual has been published by the editor of *Trade Wind* since 1972. Circulation is not known.

CHAPTER THREE

Cashing in by mail

Getting a cash refund is a simple-enough process. You find out about a refund offer, get the required labels, send them to the company, and wait for your cash return. But there are many bits and pieces of information you should be aware of before you start cashing in on your correspondence.

ABOUT FORMS

To begin with, there are two kinds of cash refunds: those that don't require offer forms and those that do. Most offers do not require forms. Unless the refund source clearly states "entry form required" or "with this coupon," you can assume that all you need are a slip of paper with your name and address and the required labels. But if a form is required and you fail to send it in, you may waste the price of a postage stamp. (Surprisingly, about 50 per cent of the form-must-accompany offers pay without forms. Just one place experience pays off, as you learn which companies will pay senders who do not have a form to submit.)

Many companies (such as Purina, Banquet, Mrs. Paul's, and French's) merely request forms; others (such as Pillsbury) always demand them. The required-form offers, which account for about 25 per cent of all cash refunds, present special problems for the refunder because often the forms are not available from local stores or newspaper or magazine ads. When this happens, the only solution is to trade forms through exchanges advertised in the refund bulletins. Most bulletins contain a classified section in which women who have extra refund forms offer to trade with you. If a required form is a particularly prized one, such as a $5.00 refund, the advertisement will usually specify the form. But generally, the ads simply say "forms traded one for one," which means that for each form you send to the address in the ad, you will receive one form. When you have twenty-five or more extra forms, these trading deals are well worth the price of the stamps needed to send for them. We mention stamps because most traders,

CASHING IN BY MAIL

> HERE'S **50¢** TO TRY
> **RICE-A-RONI WILD RICE MIX**
>
> Fill out this coupon and attach 2 box tops showing price spot from packages of Wild Rice-A-Roni. Mail to address below. We will send you 50¢.
>
> NAME
> ADDRESS
> CITY
> STATE   ZIP
>
> Mail to: Golden Grain,
> Box 1000, Rosemount, Minn. 55068
> Limit one offer per family.
> **OFFER EXPIRES JUNE 1, 1973**

This offer is used for illustration only. It is void and may not be redeemed.

since they pay for the ad and receive many time-consuming orders, ask that you send a stamped, self-addressed envelope with your request for a swap. Some also ask that you pay a *shuffling fee,* perhaps from $.10 to $.25, as compensation for their time. We've found that exchangers who do not charge a fee usually take the best forms for their own use, being less interested in repeat business than in finding forms for themselves. Those who charge a fee, on the other hand, usually strive for repeat exchanges and therefore put the needs of their customers before their own.

The scarcity of required forms encourages some unethical refunders to grab fistfuls of forms when they are available in supermarkets. After all, these people argue, extra forms can always be traded for other forms. In fact, the shortage of forms is partially a result of refunders taking more than they need and leaving none for anyone else. The honest refunder —who takes only one form, cannot find the others she needs, and has no extra forms to trade—is the person who loses out. But there is a way of solving this self-perpetuating problem. If everyone will take just one form, there will probably be enough forms to go around, and there will be less need for trading them by mail.

Frequently, official forms are not available because local grocers can't be bothered putting them on display or because the merchandise salesmen forgot to offer them to the grocer. If you let your grocer know that you are interested in refund offers and disappointed that you don't see more of them in his store, he will usually rectify the situation easily enough by asking the salesmen for them.

The company making the offer requires forms in order to predict response and, infrequently, to limit entries to a specific geographic region. (These are legitimate reasons, and after all, it's their money.) Therefore, photocopies or any other unauthorized (by the sponsor) duplication will not be accepted. As a last resort, you can write to the company and ask for a form. Some companies will mail forms, but many will not. Some who refuse your request will send, as compensation, cash-off coupons for their products. However, writing to companies for forms is a great deal of trouble and really isn't advisable unless the offer is outstanding.*

Approximately three-fourths of all cash-refund offers do not require forms, so many refunders simply avoid buying products that offer form-required refunds unless, of course, the form is readily available. (Some refund bulletins try to print only those offers requiring no form.) But although there certainly are enough offers so that this can be done, you will miss many good offers if you ignore required-form refunds.

Once you have the required form or the instruction sheet (in the case of a cash refund that doesn't ask for a form), your next step is to check the expiration date. Occasionally, offers run for indefinite periods, but most refund offers do have an expiration date. Some cash-refund offers are good for three months; some, for a year; some, for an unspecified time that we can only assume means eternity or until the sponsor decides to close the offer.

When you clip a refund ad from a newspaper or magazine, look for the expiration date first. Often, these ads will say "offer good for 90 days" but will not give a starting date. According to manufacturers, this

---

* An exception to this is Procter & Gamble, which has established an address for all form requests (Procter & Gamble, Box 432, Cincinnati, Ohio 45299). When writing to them, be certain to ask for a specific form by the offer name.

means that the offer is redeemable for ninety days from the date on the publication. You should get a pencil and a calendar, figure three months from that date, and mark it clearly on the ad. Because you will have many refund offers in the works at the same time, you cannot expect to remember these dates unless you duly note them.

Closing dates are final. A clearinghouse or sponsor rents a post-office box for each refund offer being made. When the expiration date arrives, the box is closed out, usually on the same day. All responses arriving after that date either go to a dead-letter file or are returned. Make certain that your return address is on the outside of the envelope so that if the offer has expired, you will get your letter and your labels back. (After all, these labels will be good for other offers.) If you allow from seven to ten days for mailing on every offer, you won't lose out on any refunds because of tardiness.

The next thing to look for is the restriction on duplicate refunds. The *one-per-family rule* applies to most cash refunds. If no such restriction is stated on the form, send in as many as you like; but if the form says "one per family," the manufacturer will cling tenaciously to his rule and reject duplicate entries when and if they are spotted.

Frankly, if an offer is exceptionally good, few refunders restrict themselves to one refund. They devise dozens of devious methods of skirting the restriction. For example, they will use several names at the same address, use the same name (their own) at several neighbors' addresses, or or rent a post-office box for duplicate refunds. Many play the several-names game, altering the name slightly each time: for example, Mrs. John Clever, J. Clever, J. Andrew Clever, or J. A. Cliver.

Some get permission to use the names and addresses of dozens of nonrefunder friends and even contrive codes so that the persons whose names and addresses are being used need not be bothered opening refund mail. This is easily accomplished by a slight alteration of a friend's name. If the friend's name is Mrs. Jason J. Smith, the refunder sends in offers in the name of Mrs. Jason R. Smith; as soon as her friend sees the mail, she knows that it is for the refunder.

Actually, as long as a refunder sends in just one request per envelope and sends each request on a different day, there is little chance that a sponsor or clearinghouse will spot a duplicate. The mail is handled by people, not computers; and unless an exceptionally large cash refund is involved, no effort is made to catch duplicates. One refund clearinghouse handles more than 300,000 pieces of mail daily. With such volume, it just isn't economical to cross-check every letter. However, duplicates are sometimes accidentally spotted and are, of course, rejected. Unusual names or addresses typically get caught, so if you are Mrs. Wilhelm Furtwangler of

Conshohocken, Pennsylvania, or Rondyl Leftwich of Waxahachie, Texas, don't try to pull any fast ones. Our best advice is: Honor the one-per-family ruling. There are still ways to receive many refunds from the same offer.

How? By swapping what refunders call *complete deals*. You simply attach the entry blank to the labels required, then swap the whole thing with someone else for an entry blank and set of labels you can use. You swap dollar-for-dollar value; for example, if it is a $2.00 refund offer, the other person gives you one or more complete deals equal to a $2.00 cash return. In this way, you will never send in a duplicate refund request to the sponsor and yet continue to earn money from an offer. Once again, the classified section of your refund bulletin will usually have ads from women who want to swap complete deals.

Swapping complete deals works because each family has different favorite products or uses different selective-need products such as baby food, cat food, dog food, dishwasher detergents, and patent medicines.

Check the post-office box number on each offer form. The same manufacturer may run a half-dozen similar offers on the same product at the same time. Each new box number represents a completely different offer and, therefore, can be utilized by the same family. Also compare expiration dates on seemingly identical offers. If they are different, you know you have separate offers.

ABOUT LABELS AND BOX TOPS

Now that you're positive you know what the offer form is all about, the next step in the refunding process is getting the labels, box tops, or whatever the sponsor requires. The subject of labels (admen call them *proofs of purchase* or *qualifiers*) will be discussed at length in Chapter Six, but at this point it is important to warn you against sending the wrong label with your offer. If the manufacturer asks for two endseals from his giant-sized tube of toothpaste, be certain that that is exactly what you send him. Two seals from a larger or smaller size will often be rejected. The reason, naturally, is that the manufacturer is trying to push not only a brand of toothpaste but also a size that has not been selling as well as others in the line. If the advertisement leaves room for doubt about what portion of the package is required, you can assume that the trademark is what they're after. If the package is small, take no chances; send the entire thing. Give the man what he wants, and he'll cheerfully mail you some cash.

ABOUT YOU

The next step is to identify yourself. Print your name and address on the required form or, if a form is not required, on a small sheet of white paper or a three-by-five-inch card. If you have a rubber stamp or gummed address labels, by all means use them instead. Many refunds cannot be sent or are misaddressed because of poor, illegible handwriting. Do not use abbreviations in addresses. "N. Street" could be North Street or just N Street, and both streets will often be in the same city. "Mass. Ave." may seem to be a perfectly logical abbreviation for Massachusetts Avenue, but it will undoubtedly be read as Mass Ave. Be exceedingly careful when writing out numbers; a scrawled 7 can be read as a 9 or even a 4.

Always place your complete name and address inside the envelope as well as on it. Refund clearinghouses and companies use machines to open letters, and the envelopes are immediately discarded. If your address was on the envelope only, you will not get your money. One refunder included this bit of advice in a letter to me recently. I would have written and thanked her, but her address was not on the letter, and I had thrown her envelope out with the morning trash. Apparently, the lady was more fond of giving advice than taking it.

Then there was the woman who included the following note with her refund request: "You advertise that your coffee is 'good to the last drop.' What's wrong with the last drop?" Clever, but inappropriate in a refund letter. Don't ask questions or praise the product in your letter. It is a waste of your valuable refunding time, and the clearinghouse, which is set up only to pay refunds, will never answer. Your name, address, and a simple line identifying the offer (such as "$1.00 refund for two box tops of Cruddy soap") are all that is required.

Now that your refund is in the mail, you can sit back and relax. Processing your refund, especially if it is a popular offer, takes from three to six weeks and sometimes longer. Merchandise offers take still longer to arrive and infrequently are delayed because the sponsor runs out of the offered item and has to wait for a new shipment from the makers. Also, sponsors send their refunds and merchandise via third-class mail, which is handled only after all other mail is processed. And remember, third-class mail isn't normally forwarded, so don't give a temporary address if you ever hope to see your refund.

Avid refunders estimate that from 2 to 5 per cent of their refund mail never comes back. This can be attributed to the post office losing the letter, the clearinghouse misplacing it, or the refunder's own error in sending in the wrong information. If your refund doesn't arrive within a reasonable time, recheck your own records. If you are certain you are not at fault, write to the sponsor telling him you were neglected. He'll most likely make it up to you.

CHAPTER FOUR

Money isn't everything

Cash refunds are the meat and potatoes of refunding, but the other offers are the dessert. Free-item certificates, free- or discount-merchandise offers, cents-off coupons, point coupons, trading stamps, on-label discounts, with-purchase premiums, and contests all provide the refunder with substantial savings.

CENTS-OFF CERTIFICATES

The least impressive of all the offers, yet one that can provide as much as $200.00 a year in purchase discounts, is the cents-off certificate. These offers, ranging from $.05 to $.25, are redeemable at your grocery store upon purchase of the required item.

MONEY ISN'T EVERYTHING 62

They are well worth including in your refunding efforts because they make up the difference between the prices of national brands and store brands. Nationally recognized brands cost a little more than local or store brands. Realizing this, advertisers usually give out cents-off certificates to persuade shoppers to try their brand. National manufacturers also use cents-off certificates to try out a new, lower price. If the merchandise sells better at the reduced price, the company may soon change the regular price. And thanks to a new FTC ruling, you can be sure that the offers are legitimate and not just discounts on inflated prices. The law demands that cents-off prices be figured from the ordinary price and that the regular price be stated, too.

Oddly enough, although the cents-off certificate represents the smallest refunding value, it has the most restrictions on its use. These certificates are considered by law to be a form of currency and, therefore, are carefully governed by federal regulatory agencies. It is illegal to sell these certificates. You can give them away or swap them with friends and neighbors, but selling them can get you in a lot of trouble. Furthermore, you may use the cents-off certificates for the specified product only. Talking your grocer into letting you use the certificate for a slightly different product is also basically illegal. It's also a common practice. In the mid-1950s, Safeway Markets announced that *all* coupons would be

CENTS-OFF CERTIFICATES

> **7¢** Dealer: As our agent, redeem this coupon for 7¢ on the purchase of one package of Green Giant frozen Broccoli in Cheese Sauce, Cauliflower in Cheese Sauce, Cream Style Corn, Creamed Spinach or Creamed Onions. Mail this coupon to Green Giant Company, Box 90, Le Sueur, Minnesota 56058. We will then pay you 7¢ plus 3¢ handling. This offer void in any state or locality where taxed, prohibited, or restricted by law. Fraud Clause: Any other application of this coupon constitutes fraud. Invoices proving purchases within 90 days of sufficient stock to cover coupons presented for redemption must be made available upon request. Offer expires May 31, 1973.
>
> **save 7¢**
> vegetables in special sauces
>
> on Green Giant frozen
> - Broccoli in Cheese Sauce
> - Cauliflower in Cheese Sauce
> - Cream Style Corn
> - Creamed Spinach or Creamed Onions
>
> 21-776

This offer is used for illustration only. It is void and may not be redeemed.

redeemed, whether they were applied to the specified products or not (a practice long since discontinued). Small supermarket chains have either expressed the same policy or tacitly practiced it. This can lead to some embarrassing situations, such as the incident reported by the trade paper *Supermarket News,* in which a customer pulled out a wad of coupons worth $58 to apply toward a total grocery bill of $65.

This policy occasionally backfires, especially on the independent grocery store, because the sponsor will often check the number of coupons from a store against the number of items that the grocery has purchased. In other words, if a grocer bought only two dozen cans of Fizzly Punch but took in coupons for four dozen cans, the sponsor is going to balk. When he does,

MONEY ISN'T EVERYTHING 64

the coupons are rejected, and the grocer is out their face value. However, this seldom happens to gigantic food chains because they purchase boxcar loads of an item at any one time, which makes getting more coupons than items sold highly improbable.

Here are some additional tips on using cents-off certificates: Watch those expiration dates; they are as rigid as cash-refund dates. Mark the retail price of the item on the coupon you wish to redeem. This can be a timesaver for the check-out clerk, and it can also be a money saver for you because a careless clerk may add rather than subtract the coupon discount. Always give the check-out clerk your coupons before he rings up your sale. Some stores take the amount off an item before ringing it up, while others refund the coupon value after totaling the bill. Watch carefully so that mistakes can be caught before you pay your bill. Don't try to redeem cents-off certificates at small grocery stores. Grocers receive the price of the certificate plus $.02 for handling, which is a low operating margin; so unless the grocer does a lot of business and takes in dozens of cents-off certificates, it doesn't pay him to handle them. The large chain stores are the best places for a refunder to do business, both because of the cents-off certificates and because of generally lower prices across the board.

Once you become a refunder, you will learn from experience which cents-off certificates are worth using. Because cents-off certificates are more valuable when used

MARKDOWNS

as an adjunct to your cash refunding, you will want to pay particular attention to using coupons on products that may later offer refunds. This can compound savings nicely. However, even when further rewards are not likely, a $.05 or $.10 discount on an item you can use represents a real savings.

MARKDOWNS

Another kind of purchasing discount that you should know about is the *markdown*. The amount of the markdown will usually be printed on the package, for

This offer is used for illustration only. It is void and may not be redeemed.

example, "special offer—25 cents off the regular price." This is essentially the same as a cents-off certificate, but without the bother of handling certificates. Like the cents-off certificates, the markdown discounts are most valuable if they appear on national brands that offer cash refunds as well. The manufacturer has sold the merchandise to the storekeeper at a $.25 reduction and is asking him to pass the saving on to you. Try to find out what the regular price was; this will help you avoid being taken by a grocer who would rather pocket the discount than pass it along. With new FDA rules (see Glossary), this deceptive practice is much less common, but it still happens.

Best of all, there is what refunders call the *triple bonanza*. You get a $.50 product marked down by $.15, then use a $.20 coupon to buy it, and finally send in the box top on another offer and get back $.50. In short, the manufacturer has paid you $.35 and given you the product free besides. Improbable as it may seem, triple bonanzas are frequently offered.

FREE-MERCHANDISE OFFERS

Free-merchandise offers may not be as satisfying as cash in hand, but they frequently represent a much greater value. There are always from 200 to 500 such offers in process at any given time. These merchandise offers used to be noted for

FREE-MERCHANDISE OFFERS

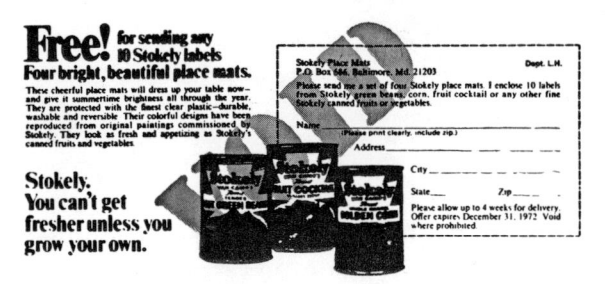

This offer is used for illustration only. It is void and may not be redeemed.

lack of quality and value, but their image has changed in the last two decades. Today you will find more expensive, higher-quality merchandise being offered: binoculars, electric coffeepots, bathroom scales, silverware, jewelry, cooking utensils, books, children's furniture, mechanical toys, electric blankets, fine china, and dozens of other useful products. Nearly every product offered is a nationally known brand, such as Cosco baby furniture, RCA radios, Polaroid cameras or Melmac dishes. Often, this merchandise is not yet available in stores or, if available, carries a much higher price tag than the offer would lead you to believe. Normally, the retail price is stated on the offer blank ("a value of $7.00"). You can depend on the accuracy of the stated value because misrepresentation of the item's value constitutes fraud.

Because the free merchandise tends to be of real value, the number of labels, endseals, or box tops required for each item is considerable. Many refunders shy away from such offers because their purchases of

MONEY ISN'T EVERYTHING 68

a cereal or soap will be restricted for weeks and even months, thus forcing them to miss out on any excellent cash-refund offers that crop up during that time span. But buying the product isn't the only way to get labels. A refunder can buy labels through many different sources advertised in refund bulletins, swap other labels to get them, or scrounge them from friends.

CASH-PLUS OFFERS

An even more popular merchandise offer is one in which you send in cash plus labels to obtain an item at a drastically reduced price. Some fields, such as the cereal industry, are inundated with this kind of offer. Because the sponsor makes no profit on the merchandise, and because he buys in huge lots (as many as a million items), the price you pay is usually less than half the retail price.

This offer is used for illustration only. It is void and may not be redeemed.

Get a $24.95 Fondue pot for only $13.95.

Please send me_____ West Bend electric Fondue pots. I enclose $13.95 (check or money order) payable to Clam Fondue Offer plus the cap liner from one bottle of Planters Oil and the ingredient panel from one package of Howard Johnson's Tendersweet Fried Clams for each pot. Allow 4 to 6 weeks for delivery. Offer good only in U.S.A. Offer expires June 30, 1973. Void where prohibited or restricted.

Name_____

Address_____

City_____ State_____ Zip_____
☐ Pimento red
☐ Cheddar yellow

Send to Clam Fondue Offer, Box 218, Rockfield, Wisconsin, 53077.
Orders without zip code cannot be accepted. © 1972, Howard Johnson Co.

These special-price offers usually have no closing date. If the offer has outlived the supply of the merchandise being offered, the sponsor more often than not will give you a choice of current product offerings of equal value. Recently, there has been a trend toward shorter-term offers, but the advertisement announcing the offer will always tip you off by such qualifying phrases as "for a limited time only" or "while the supply lasts."

Here are a few rules you should know about sending money through the mails: Always tape coins between two pieces of cardboard so that the contour of the coin cannot be felt from the outside of the envelope. Dollar bills should be placed inside a sheet of paper. Although postal authorities work diligently at keeping mail theft to a minimum, it still occurs, especially in the case of loose cash in envelopes. For merchandise purchases of $2.00 or more, you should avoid possible loss by sending a check. In this way, if you fail to receive your premium, you'll have the canceled check as proof you sent in the order.

Do not send postage stamps in lieu of money. For some reason, many people think of stamps as a form of cash. But merchandisers and clearinghouses don't share this opinion. Remember, these businesses use precanceled stamping machines for all letters and therefore have no need of loose stamps. Often the advertisement will say "no stamps accepted," but even if this is not spelled out, you can bank on getting your stamps back with a brief request for cash or money orders, in which case you will have wasted your postage.

POINT COUPONS

Both trading-stamp and point-coupon offers are promotional gimmicks contrived to build repeat business. In the case of trading stamps, the customer will return to the same store in order to fill her redemption books. In the case of point coupons, the customer must continue to purchase the same company's products in order to accumulate coupon points. In both cases, the consumer's goal is to get merchandise for little or no outlay of cash.

Most of the rules that apply to merchandise offers apply equally to point coupons. Instead of saving a few labels, you collect point coupons from packages and containers; and instead of having one gift to save for, you can choose your gift from a catalog of excellent merchandise. Furthermore, the coupons, even very old ones, continue to be redeemable, especially when mixed with a few recent ones when sent in.

The Betty Crocker coupon plan is the largest and oldest in the United States. It was begun in 1930 when an employee came up with the idea of offering a free teaspoon to generate brand loyalty. Today, Betty Crocker coupons are available on all fifty General Mills bread and cereal products. Offering mostly kitchenware in their catalog, General Mills uses the cash-plus-coupons method. For example, you can get a Dutch oven for $5.75 and 7 coupons. They also offer the option of more coupons and less cash. In the case of the Dutch oven, you can also send $5.00 and 75 coupons. The fewer-coupons-more-cash option seems to have a slight value edge over the more-coupons option, and from a refunder's point of view, it isn't as binding on purchasing power.

Point-coupon offers have proven particularly effective for product lines that do not normally make other kinds of refund offers. In the cigarette industry, for example, Brown & Williams Tobacco Corporation has profited for nearly forty years largely because they are one of the few companies in the industry that offer coupons. In 1960, Brown & Williams came out with Belair cigarettes as a sales mate to their well-established Raleigh brand. The public was not overwhelmingly impressed with Belair cigarettes until 1962, when the Raleigh coupon was added; then sales shot up 229 per cent. It is interesting to note that now that television advertising of cigarettes has been banned, more tobacco companies are looking to refund offers as sales incentives. In fact, this industry may soon join the ranks of the leading refunding companies.

Because of laws in some states (such as Wisconsin and Wyoming) that point coupons must be redeemable for cash, coupon companies in every state frequently allow consumers the option of redeeming coupons for cash rather than merchandise. With few exceptions, however, the merchandise redemption represents a far better value than cash redemption.

Point couponing takes a concerted effort and will tend to scatter your shot at cash refunding. But if your main reason for refunding is to make money in order to buy merchandise, you can save a great deal by skipping the cash approach and heading straight for the goodies with point coupons in hand. The best way to see if point couponing meets your needs is to send for a few of the many point-coupon catalogs. The following list of point-coupon programs is by no means complete, but it does include most of the larger programs that have national followings.

Food and Consumable Products Plans

BONUS GIFTS, P.O. Box 2334, Los Angeles, California 90054.

Although it is presently restricted to the East Coast and Southwest, this fairly new organization shows signs of becoming national. Coupons come with a wide range of products from soap to cigarettes. A list of the companies involved and a merchandise catalog are available by writing to Bonus Gifts.

GENERAL MILLS, 400 Second Avenue South, Minneapolis, Minnesota 55440.

This is the famous Betty Crocker plan, offering coupons with nearly seventy different General Mills products. Send for a free club catalog that lists the dozens of high-quality items available, including silverware, kitchen appliances, cooking utensils, and even camping gear. Special deals can also be arranged for more expensive items such as school buses, cars, organs, and anything else a group might want to bargain for.

GIFT STARS, INC., Box 1155, Minneapolis, Minnesota 55440.

A relative newcomer to the point-coupon business, Gift Stars offers a fine assortment of merchandise. The coupons are found on a wide assortment of products from La Choy chinese foods to Lay's potato chips. A list of products offering Gift Stars coupons is available with the catalog. Coupons can be combined with trading stamps for redemption at participating centers, or the point coupons can be turned in for cash.

GOLD CIRCLE, Box 1308, Salina, Kansas 67401.

A wide assortment of household merchandise is offered in Gooch's catalog with Gold Circle and Red Circle coupons. Gooch includes their coupons with their wide range of food products and animal feeds.

PLEE-ZING COUPONS, 1903 Harrison Street, Evanston, Illinois 60201.

Virtually all Plee-Zing brand products carry point coupons. They are redeemable directly from the company, which does not utilize trading-stamp chains.

QUIK-SAVE, P.O. Box 15150, St. Louis, Missouri 63110.

This is another point-coupon program that is offered by several different companies' products. Quik-Save has a medium-range distribution. Write to them for a list of producers offering the coupons and merchandise descriptions.

RED SCISSORS, INC., 12715-B State Highway 55, Minneapolis, Minnesota 55427.

These coupons can be found on a variety of products, including Borden's condensed milk and Tetley tea. Redemption is accomplished in one of two ways: You can trade the point coupons in for gifts at any of nearly a hundred trading-stamp companies, or you can trade them in for cash, at .3 cents per point. Red Scissors also provides special programs and products for organizations. A list of participating trading-stamp companies can be obtained by writing to Red Scissors.

Tobacco Company Plans

BANDWAGON USA, Box 2814, Philadelphia, Pennsylvania 19122.

You get these coupons with Phillies and other cigars made by Bayuk Cigars, Inc. Write and ask them for their gift catalog.

BROWN & WILLIAMS TOBACCO CORP., Box 903, Louisville, Kentucky 40201.

This is the oldest plan in the tobacco industry. Coupons come with Raleigh and Belair cigarettes. Write to Brown & Williams for their gift catalog.

BUSINESS INCENTIVES, INC., Larus and Brothers Co., 7630 East Bush Lake Road, Minneapolis, Minnesota 55435.

You will get these coupons with Domino cigarettes. A catalog of redeemable merchandise is available.

HAVATAMPA, P.O. Box 1261, Tampa, Florida 33601.

Coupons come with Havatampa cigars. Send for the gift catalog.

LUXURY MERCHANDISE CO., P.O. Box 1214, Minneapolis, Minnesota 55440.

These coupons are offered by Chesterfield cigarettes. A gift catalog is available upon request.

SWIFT GIFT DIVIDEND COUPONS, P.O. Box 41666, Cincinnati, Ohio 45241.

Coupons are given with Alpine and Galaxy cigarettes. Write for a catalog describing the gifts available.

TRADING STAMPS

Whereas point-coupon offers (like all other refund-offer methods) are paid for out of the general advertising budget of the sponsoring company and thus represent a true saving to consumers, trading stamps (although they appear to be the same as point coupons) do not. Economists say most trading stamps (such as S&H, Top Value, and Blue Chip) give 2.5 cents worth of purchasing power for every dollar's worth of purchases. All but .5 cents of this value comes out of the pocket of the storekeeper or filling station owner who gives out the stamps. Obviously, the storekeeper must make up this 2 per cent expense somewhere, and his prices are the logical place to do it. Instead of raising all prices 2 per cent, the storekeeper may simply not run specials, or he may raise prices inconspicuously on a few items. However it is accomplished, you can be fairly sure the customer ends up paying a goodly portion of the 2.5 cent gift. In essence, trading stamps represent a direct tax on every shopper. Thus, the shopper must save the stamps or pay a penalty for frequenting the store.

Trading-stamp companies, of course, sing a very different tune. They claim that any store which gives stamps will realize a large-enough increase in business to more than compensate for the cost of the stamps and that, therefore, the customer doesn't pay anything extra for this premium. However, since trading stamps are no longer in great demand, we doubt that giving stamps actually lures in great hordes of new customers.

At one time in the not-too-distant past, 80 per cent of all American women saved trading stamps; but as inflation climbed, the use of trading stamps faltered and is now steadily declining in popularity. The number of trading-stamp companies has dwindled from close to 2,000 a little over a decade ago to just 200 in 1973. Objections to the direct cost increase have been so great that sixteen states now have laws requiring grocers to offer a discount at the check-out counter equal to the cash value of the trading stamps if a customer elects not to accept them.

Many women continue to defend trading stamps on the premise they represent a kind of forced savings. After a few months of shopping at a store that offers stamps, the shopper ends up with a gift she would not have saved for otherwise. After all, don't these companies give out $800 million in free merchandise each year? This argument is a rather blatant admission that the consumer cannot handle money well enough to save without being forced into it.

On the other hand, you wouldn't be a thrifty shopper if you didn't take stamps whenever they are available from a store or business that you are going to deal with anyway. The trading-stamp companies make money only because most of the stamps they give away are never redeemed.

Actually, when it comes to saving stamps, you, as a refunder, have an advantage that most housewives lack. That is, you have access to refund bulletin ads that will put you in touch with other refunders who will barter with you for those stamps. They will often give you refund forms or coupons for the stamps or swap one kind of stamp for another. You can probably find someone in your own city who makes a business of exchanging trading stamps. In this way, you can amass enough of a single type to cash in on worthwhile merchandise.

A final bit of advice on trading stamps:

Save for the higher-priced items. Studies have shown that you get less value on blankets, sheets, bowls, and small appliances than you do on major merchandise such as silverware, china, and electric skillets.

In short, the smart refunder should have no illusions about trading stamps. After all, saving money is the entire rationale behind refunding, so shopping at stores that offer reasonable low prices must be part of that goal. You can save money by saving trading stamps, but you can also lose money if you always shop at the same store just to collect stamps.

CHAPTER FIVE

Cash in your trash

As a refunder, the ecologists will love you because you won't be polluting the environment with a lot of trash. Instead, you'll hoard trash and stockpile it in your basement.

WHAT IS A TRASH TROVE AND WHY DO YOU NEED ONE

Companies that have a history of making refund offers can be depended upon to make offers in the future. By anticipating the offers, you can make a great deal more on refunding than you could by merely buying the product while the offer is running. If you save labels and the inner seals from instant coffee jars, you will be ready to make money on an offer from the day it is introduced.

For the woman who does not establish a trash trove or label library, refunding can become somewhat awkward. If one week before an expiration date she hears about an offer of $3.00 for twelve bean soup can labels, she will have to rush out and buy all twelve cans at one time, peel off the labels and send them in. She'll get her refund to be sure, but she'll have a lot of bean soup to use up. Furthermore, buying large quantities of a product at one time in order to take advantage of a current offer is out of the question for some refunders' budgets.

Your trash trove need not be so large that it infringes on you family's living space. Although it is probably best to keep all boxes, labels, and jar caps, few refunders do. By being selective and saving only those brand containers that you know from experience will be worthwhile, your trash trove can be kept within bounds.

In general, the beginning refunder should shop by company names rather than brand names. Certain companies provide cash-refund and merchandise offers on every one of their products from time to time and you can seldom go astray by stocking up on their products. Rather than memorize lists of brands, look for the company name on the package. It would take you years if you did try to familiarize yourself with all the brand names produced by every one of these companies. For example, General Foods produces a hodgepodge of

WHAT IS A TRASH TROVE?

unrelated brands, including Birds Eye frozen foods, Jell-O, Maxwell House coffee, Minute Rice, Gaines dog food, Good Seasons, Swansdown, Sanka, and Log Cabin syrup. All are occasionally involved in refund offers.

The following fourteen companies are the largest ones that make regular offers on virtually every one of their products. (At the end of this chapter, we've also included lists of brand names that should be represented in your trash trove.) You will do well to save labels and boxes from every one of these.

Best Foods
Borden
Campbell
French's
General Foods
General Mills
Green Giant

Kraft Foods
Lever Brothers
Lipton
Pillsbury
Procter & Gamble
Standard Brands
Stokely-Van Camp

Many other companies make sporadic refund offers that you will learn through experience, but you may decide not to include them in your trash trove because of their uncertain returns.

Store all labels from canned products and all inner seals, cap liners, and labels from jars and bottles. Save the entire container of all products in soft packages (boxes and bags). These are fairly simple to store if you slit the boxes open so that they will lie flat and then bind them together with string. Some refunders, in a valiant attempt at saving storage space, attempt to second-guess what part of a package the sponsoring company will request. They are often wrong. Also, manufacturers switch around in asking for one part or another because they want to dissuade consumers from stockpiling parts of their package. Needless to say, their logic is erroneous. One company recently had a half-dozen refund offers out of the same product, and each offer asked for a different part of the package. The refunder who saved the entire box was able to collect six times on a single container. So save the entire box, and you might be able to cash in on the top, bottom, net weight marking, size marker, ingredients listing, guarantee statement, or all the above.

You should also keep a few bread, doughnut, ice cream, egg, meat, and cookie containers on hand. Not that their manufacturers might offer refunds (because most such products are produced at local levels by small firms), but other manufacturers might ask for them. Frequently, a sponsor will want you to try their product along with something else, for example, their tea with any brand of cookies or their canned chili with any brand of crackers. In such cases, you will need the manufacturer's label plus the label of the other item, so save a few miscellaneous packages for these offbeat requests.

Once you establish your trash trove, you'll want to add as many labels and boxes to your holdings as possible. You can do this not only by careful selection of the foods you buy for your own family but also looking elsewhere for valuable qualifying labels. Among the best sources of extra packages are a refunder's relatives and friends. Ask them not to throw out any brand-name containers until you make your once-a-week visit to reap the trash harvest. (If you gratefully acknowledge their help with an occasional gift obtained from a merchandise offer, they will stay in your corner and keep on supplying you with labels.)

Stop in occasionally at laundromats and laundry rooms of apartment complexes to pick up all the empty soap boxes you'll need. If you work or have friends who work at restaurants, hospitals, nursing homes, or motels, draw on their vast consumption for labels and boxes. And although it sounds repulsive, some refunders even make regular pilgrimages to the city dump to retrieve labels. You should keep an eye on the classified section of your refunders' bulletin for ads from people selling *qualifiers* (meaning labels). These generally sell for from $.01 to $.07 each, depending on the product's value; thus, there isn't much advantage to buying or selling them unless you plan to deal in volumes.

Also watch your refund bulletin for regional offers. If you see that a refund is being made on a product in California and Oregon and you live in New York, start saving your labels. Regional offers are usually shifted from state to state or expanded to national status.

A word of warning: When you spot a refund offer, go to the store and see if the present labels are the same as those in your collection. Manufacturers occasionally change their containers, and they may or may not accept old labels on new refund offers. Also, read the offer form carefully. If it says "with the special label from . . .," you can be reasonably sure that the manufacturer has printed special labels and will not grant you a refund on the regular one. But because changing a label is expensive, companies do not do it often, so most of the time your trash collection is as good as gold.

STARTING AND STORING YOUR TRASH TROVE

To help you get your trash trove started, we've compiled a list of labels you should save because they have proved to be refundable in recent years. We've included some suggestions on removing and storing these labels and packages.

Getting the labels off plastic and glass containers is a trick that deserves a brief mention. Soak the entire container in a pan of cold water for several hours to dissolve the glue on the label. To remove can labels, simply slide a knife down any portion of the label that is not glued (next to the seam

STARTING YOUR TRASH TROVE

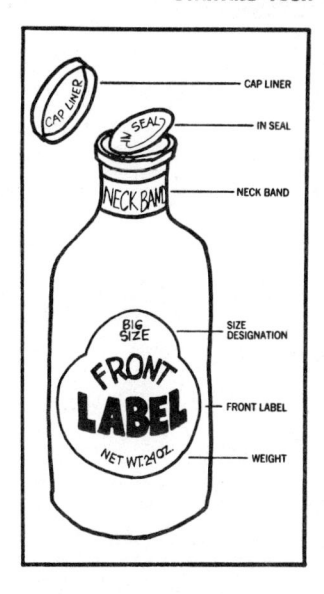

is best); you can then unwrap the label, by peeling it away from the can slowly.

Bottled Cleaning Products
Save front *and* back labels. Labels can be cut off plastic bottles.

Ajax liquid (front, back)
Austin's (front)
Cold Water All liquid (front, back)
Clorox (net contents marker)
Dove liquid (front, back)
Downy fabric softener (front, back)
Final Touch fabric softener (front, back)
Ivory liquid (front)
Joy liquid (front)
Lux liquid (front, back)

Mr. Clean (front)
Palmolive liquid (front)
Sta-Puf
Sweetheart (front)
Thrill liquid (front)
Top Job (front)
Wisk (front, back)

Bottled Drug and Cosmetic Products
Corn Huskers lotion (front)
Enden liquid shampoo (front)
Rejoice shampoo (neckband)
Scope mouthwash (front)

Bottled Food Products
Patient soaking is required to remove these labels. Save front *and* back labels (if any) *and* neckbands (if any). File them in small envelopes in alphabetical order (by brand name) and store them in a box. Write the product size and variety identification, if needed, on the neckband. We've given the specific parts of the labels that were asked for in past offers.

A1 steak sauce (neckband)
Bennett's chili sauce (neckband)
Bernsteins' dressings (neckband)
Blue Plate (front)
Brooks catsup (front)
Canada Dry (front, neckband)
Crisco oil (front)
Crosse & Blackwell (front)
Don the Beachcomber (front, neckband)
Frenchette dressings (front)
Heinz (front, neckband)
Hellmann's dressings (front, back)

STARTING YOUR TRASH TROVE

Hellmann's mayonnaise
Hunt's catsups (front, neckband)
Kraft barbecue sauce (neckband)
Kraft dressings (neckband, front)
Kraft jellies (front)
Kraft mayonnaise (front)
Kraft oil (front)
Log Cabin (cap liner, front)
Mayonette Gold
Miracle Whip dressing (front)
Mrs. Butterworth's (capliner, front)
Old Dutch dressings (front)
Open Pit barbecue sauce (neck)
Peter Pan peanut butter (front)
Salad Bowl dressing (front)
Skippy peanut butter (front)
Smucker's (front)
Staley fondue oil (front)
Vermont Maid syrup (front)
Vogeler's mayonnaise
Welch's jellies (front)
Wesson oil (front)
Wish-Bone dressings (neckband, front)

Boxed Cleaning Products
All (box top, net weight, others)
Axion (box top)
Biz (box top, net weight)
Bold (box top, net weight)
Breeze (box top, net weight)
Brillo (net weight)
Cascade dishwasher detergent (box top, net weight)
Cheer (box top, net weight)
Dash (box top, net weight, size designation)
Diaper Sweet (box top)

CASH IN YOUR TRASH

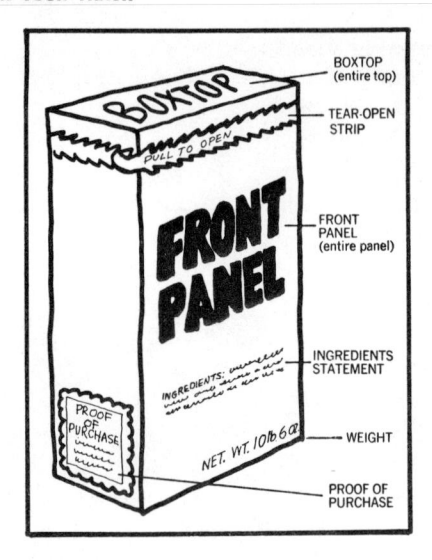

Diagram of a box with labels: BOXTOP (entire top), TEAR-OPEN STRIP, FRONT PANEL (entire panel), INGREDIENTS STATEMENT, WEIGHT, PROOF OF PURCHASE

Dreft (baby picture front)
Fab (net weight)
Finish dishwasher detergent (box top)
Gain (net weight)
Ivory Flakes (box top, net weight)
Ivory Snow (box top, net weight, size)
Oxydol (box top, net weight)
Rinso (box top)
Salvo (box top)
Spic and Span
Surf (box top)
Tide (box top, net weight)

Boxed Drug and Cosmetic Products
In this case, the box is more accurately described as a carton. Flatten it, and save the entire thing.

Anacin
Ban deodorant

Carefree tampons
Close-Up toothpaste
Colgate toothpaste
Crest toothpaste
Efferdent
Excedrin
Fems (proof of purchase)
Gleem toothpaste
Head & Shoulders shampoo
Kleenex (proof of purchase)
Kotex (proof of purchase)
Lustre-Creme shampoo
Modess
Pampers diapers
Pertussin cough syrup (box top)
Prell shampoo
Pristeen
Puffs (open flap, overwrap)
Softique bath oil (box top)
Tender Touch bath oil (box top)
Ultra Brite toothpaste
Vanquish
Vote toothpaste

Boxed Food Products

Boxes can be flattened and stored. Saving the entire box is usually not necessary *if* you know what portion the sponsor usually calls for and *if* the sponsor doesn't make a switch. But remember that if you store the entire carton, you may get two or three proofs from one box.

Alba instant milk (front, open end flap)
Aunt Jemima sticks (ingredient panel)
Blue Bonnet (front)
Borden's (box top)

CASH IN YOUR TRASH

Brilliant
Buitoni (front)
Cacklebird (box top)
Chef Boy-Ar-Dee (box top)
Chef Boy-Ar-Dee frozen
Chex cereals (box top, proof of purchase)
Del Monte snack packs (front, open end flap)
Delmonico dinners (box top)
Durkee (front, box top)
Fleischmann's margarines (open end flap)
French's (front, box top, variety)
Gaines pet foods (front, box top, net weight, ingredient panel)
Golden Grain (box top)
Gorton's (front, variety, open end flap)
Green Giant (front, ingredient panel, trademark, open end flap)
Imperial margarines (front, ingredient panel, open end flap)
Jiffy (front)
John's pizza (front, back)
Johnston's pies (front)
Kellogg's cereals (box top, proof of purchase)
Kordite (front, back, proof of purchase)
Kraft (front, box top)
Kraft frozen (trademark variety)
Lambrecht (ingredient panel)
Land O'Lakes (trademark, "US Seal")
Lipton (front, box top, ingredient panel)
Martha Gooch (net weight)
Morton (front, box top, ingredient panel)
Mrs. Filbert's (front, trademark, open end flap)
Mrs. Paul's (front, ingredient panel)

Nabisco (box top)
Nucoa margarine (front)
On-Cor (front, ingredient panel)
Pillsbury (front, box top, ingredient panel, net weight)
Post cereals (box top, proof of purchase)
Quaker (box top, proof of purchase)
Royal (front)
Stouffer's (front)
Taste O'Sea (trademark, variety)
Uncle Ben's (box top)

Canned Food Products

The labels from canned products are easy to store. Flatten them and put them in Manila envelopes, file folders, or boxes. You'll find it helpful to arrange them in alphabetical order by brand name. Note that some of these products are "canned" in glass jars.

Alpo pet foods
Armour
Aunt Millie's
Aunt Nellie's
Austex
Beech-Nut baby foods
B in B mushrooms
Betty Crocker frosting
Bunker Hill
Campbell
Chef Boy-Ar-Dee
Chicken of the Sea tuna
Chun King
College Inn
Comstock
Contadina

CASH IN YOUR TRASH

Crosse & Blackwell
Delmonico spaghetti sauce
Del Monte
Diet Delight
Dole
Doxsee
Friskies pet foods
Gerber baby foods
Gold Seal pet foods
Great American
Green Giant
Hanover
Hawaiian Punch juices
Heinz baby foods, soups
Hi-C juices
Hill's pet foods
Hunt's
Joan of Arc
Krey
La Choy
Libby's
Musselman's
Old Southern
Pillsbury frosting
Progresso soups
Purina pet foods
Purr cat foods
Puss'n Boots cat foods
Ragu spaghetti sauce
Star-Kist tuna
Stokely-Van Camp
Swanson
Thank You
Three Diamonds
Welch's juices
Wilson canned meats

STARTING YOUR TRASH TROVE

Coffee
Save the inner seal *and* label on all instant coffees, teas, and instant beverages in jars. On ground coffee, save the entire bag; on cans, save the plastic lid. When saving inner seals, inserts, or portions that do not show the product name or identification (such as net weight), *write* the identification on the back when you remove it.

Cigarettes
Save the entire package. Most offers usually ask for either the bottom panels or the closure seals.

Miscellaneous
Birds Eye frozen juices (metal can ends)
Birds Eye Cool Whip (sides)
Borden Biscuits (can label)
Chocks vitamins (card)
Dannon yogurt (lids)
Famo flour (bag bottom)
Funny Face (envelope)
Kool-Aid (envelope)
Listerine (outer wrapper, proof of purchase)
Minute Maid juice (tear strips)
Nestle Quik (code numbers)
One Step Wax (cap)
Pillsbury flour (bag bottom)
Rath canned meats (inserts)
Wyler's soup (envelopes)

Soft Drinks
Save proof-of-purchase seals from the cartons (if any). In all cases, save bottle caps

and watch especially for any imprints on cap liners.

Seasoning and Gravy Mixes
Save the outer box (if any); otherwise save the envelope.

Wrapped Bar Soaps
Camay
Dial
Dove
Lava
Lifebuoy
Lux
Palmolive
Phase III
Safeguard
Sweetheart
Zest

Wrapped Food Products
Remove the wrapper so that it can be stored flat. These are particularly difficult to flatten; it will help if you cut off and discard unprinted ends (if possible). Bag-type wrappers are included in this group.

Armour parti style ham (front)
Bar S Bounty (front, trademark)
Borden cheeses (front)
Hershey's chips (bags)
Kraft cheeses (front)
M & M/Mars candies (bags)
Morrell ham (front)
Nestle's chips (bags)
Pennsylvania Dutch (bags)

Sugardale (front, trademark)
Superior (front, trademark)
Swift's

Wrapped Paper Products
Bounty paper towels
Charmin bathroom tissue
Kleenex (proof of purchase)
Lady Scott
ScotTissues (proof of purchase)
ScotTowels (proof of purchase)
Viva towels (proof of purchase)
White Cloud bath tissue

CHAPTER SIX

You gotta get organized

If you've read this far into the book and haven't realized that refunding can be complicated, then you haven't been paying attention. Any avid refunder has hundreds of labels and boxes stacked up around her, and she has a hundred or more cash offers, a hundred or so merchandise offers, and scads of cents-off certificates in front of her. She has noted those critical expiration dates on nearly every offer. But to succeed at refunding, she must make some order out of all the chaos around her.

Getting organized is merely a matter of having everything where you can find it when you want it. Every refunder concocts her own formula for organization, and although some look like Rube Goldberg drew up the plans, they seem to work relatively well. We believe that you should approach your refunding as you would a business. The organization of any business can be judged in time saved; therefore, the best systems are those that take the least amount of time and care. In this chapter, we will discuss systems that seem to fulfill all these requirements.

SUPPLIES

The first thing you will need is a rubber stamp with your name and address printed on it or some of those inexpensive gummed address labels sold through mail-order houses. You'll save hundreds of minutes each month if you don't have to write out your address twenty times a day. Also, remember that poor handwriting is the cause of many cases of misaddressed and lost refunds.

Buy a batch of the cheapest envelopes you can find, both letter and legal size, and be sure the glue sticks. (You won't save any money if you have to use Scotch tape to seal the envelopes.) Stock up on pencils, pens, and felt-tip marking pens. Get yourself some three-by-five-inch cards, three shoe or cheese boxes, some clear tape, a stapler, some lined paper for record keeping, and you're ready for business.

SPACE

Now find yourself a place away from the mainstream of family traffic (if that's possible). You will want to keep all your refunding paraphernalia in one spot, so look for an area with a small table, a chair, and enough space around it to stack up the cardboard boxes containing your trash trove. If space is a problem, steal a compartment from your kitchen cabinets and use your kitchen table as a workbench. (Actually, many refunders prefer this approach.)

ORGANIZATION

Place the three shoe boxes in front of you and get out all the offer blanks you've been collecting. In the first box, place all your cash-refund and free-merchandise offer blanks. Arrange them in one of the following ways: (1) dated offers by month of expiration and undated offers in alphabetical order, (2) all in alphabetical order, or (3) in sections according to product type (breads, cakes, complete dinners, meats, milk products, vegetables, paper products, toiletries, and so on). Do the same thing in the second box, which will be for cents-off certificates. The third box should be reserved for merchandise offers that require cash. If you're going to take an occasional fling at drawings and sweepstakes, set up a fourth shoe box just for those entry blanks.

As you place each offer announcement or official entry blank in its proper box and category, circle the expiration date and try to arrange the shortest-term offers toward the front of each section. Get in the habit immediately of getting rid of expired offers every time you go through your files.

Next set up your trash trove or label files. Use brand names as categories, rather than company names or product types. In other words, have a category for Betty Crocker cake mix, not just one for General Mills or cakes. Small grocery bags serve well for storing flattened-out boxes. For labels and inner seals, use large nine-by-twelve Manila envelopes. Use pencil (rather than pen) to mark the envelope so that you can erase the category and use the same envelope year after year. Arrange your trash trove categories alphabetically in cardboard boxes.

PROCEDURES

Your *modus operandi* is the next thing you'll want to establish. You'll need to get into a routine so familiar that refunding becomes second nature to you.

When your refund bulletin comes in, scan the columns of offers, putting an X in front of any item that promises a good return on something your family might consume. Go down the offer column a second time, and place a second X next to any offer that asks for an official blank; then go to your offer shoe box to see if you have any of the official entry blanks for these XX offers. Pull out all these blanks, and set them aside for the moment.

Now, rummage through your trash trove in search of the appropriate labels for any of the offers listed. If you have all the labels required, fill out a card immediately, slip the labels into an envelope, and mail them right away. If you have some labels, set them aside. Repeat this process with the XX offers for which you have both official entry blanks and labels. Send these immediately also. By handling these offers as soon as you can, you avoid confusion later.

Go through your offer box once again, this time looking for offers with pressing expiration dates on items you could use in the foreseeable future. Pull these out, and match them up with the appropriate label or box top from your trash trove, and mail them.

Now, if you go back to your refund bulletin and the offers from your shoe box, you'll note many offers that you would take advantage of if only you had the required labels. So, get those labels and your refund. Plan your week's grocery shopping right then and there, trying to include at least one refund item for every meal and for all paper products and toiletries. Your shopping list should include the brand names, sizes, amounts of refunds, and any unusual required package marks (such as a gold seal). The list might look like this:

2 Sparkle toothpaste, family size, red star and flap, 50¢ R*
3 King Hadley meat pies, ingredients list, $1 R
1 Yummy chicken casserole, giant size, 75¢ R

Note that this list includes the portion of the package required for a refund. It is important for you to have this information when shopping so that you can be sure the package you buy meets the offer requirement. If, for example, the Sparkle toothpaste manufacturer changed labels to red stars on end flaps and your supermarket still has nothing but the old packages, you can shop elsewhere or wait for the packages that will give a refund.

It is important to note the amount you are to receive on the shopping list. Why? Because not all refund offers are worth the trouble. Some frozen complete dinners, for example, give $.50 off on the purchase of two; but a close inspection of various frozen dinners might reveal that the refunding company charges $.20 more per dinner than its competitor, which means that you'll pay $.40 more plus $.08 on postage and get back only $.50. This doesn't happen often, but if you remember to glance at the prices each time you shop, it won't happen at all.

Once you get the hang of this system,

---

*R is for refund.

you can develop your own brand of shorthand, for example: "2 Sparkle tooth, FS, Red Star E FL, 50R," which means "Sparkle toothpaste, family size, red star, end flap, $.50 refund."

After you've made up your shopping list, thumb through your cents-off certificates. Try to match each cash-refund item on the list with a cents-off certificate; then place an asterisk on the shopping list for each item with a cents-off certificate, attach the certificates to your list with a paper clip, and you're on your way to the grocery store.

Should you get all the labels you need for a cash refund in one shopping trip? Ideally, yes. By buying the three or four cans of the same beans at one time, you can make life less complicated for yourself and send for your refund as soon as you get home. Also, by the next time you go shopping, the expiration date might be up, or the grocer might be out of the product you need.

On the other hand, your budget may not be able to stand the strain until after you've built up reserve funds from your refunding. So if you just can't afford to stockpile a few products, don't worry about it. Stick with the offers that have expiration dates at least six weeks away, and when you get home from a shopping expedition, add the items you still need to next week's shopping list immediately so that you don't forget what you are working toward.

If you do decide to do a little buying ahead and want to send for your refund right away, you'll need to know a few tricks of package marking. Use a felt-tip marking pen and plain gummed label or adhesive tape to write the name of the product on the top of the can so you'll know what you have in your pantry. Many items (such as margarine and opened, inner-seal-removed coffee) can be stored indefinitely in your freezer. Heavy paper packages, such as cereal and soap boxes, are made of layered paper. With a little practice and a sharp knife or razor blade, you can learn to peel off the outer layer, which is the printed label, and not puncture the box. This will also save you postage because the envelope will weigh less.

Always plan an extra day's meals per week. This is essential because the brands that carry refund offers are not always in stock. Other refunders may have bought out the stock; it may not be carried by the store where you shop; or only the old packages may be on the shelves. You will often have to revise your list as you shop, so having those extra meals planned will come in handy. And if all the brands you're after are available, it can't hurt to have a one-day head start on your next shopping list.

It is smart to shop in several major grocery stores. Each store makes its own decisions about what brands it will keep on hand, so you can't always find every brand in every store. By shopping at different stores, you improve your chances of taking advantage of every current offer.

KEEPING RECORDS

Keep records of every offer you send out and every refund you receive. This record keeping is your only way of knowing whether a company actually sends you your refund. And since the money tends to trickle in a little each day and get lost in the household money, this is the only way to keep track of how much money your refunding efforts are earning you. The bookkeeping need not be complicated. List the date the offer was sent, the amount of the refund, the company and brand names, and the address or box number and leave a space to fill in the date the refund comes in. The address or box number of the offer is important because you will want to go through your record book every two or three months and send off a small note to any company or clearinghouse that has not come through with your refund. Sending a due bill to the company or clearinghouse is only practical if the offer has not yet expired and if the refund is large enough to be worth the investment of another stamp.

Occasionally, no matter how carefully you prepare and send off your request, you will not get your refund. Refunders tell us that about 5 out of every 100 refunds never materialize. Blame the post office for losing your letter, the clearinghouse for misplacing it or sending it to the wrong address, or yourself for possibly filling out the request incorrectly or sending in the wrong labels. Then chalk it up to the cost of doing business, and forget about it. Considering your low overhead and high profit margin, 5 per cent is not a great loss factor.

If you can afford to keep all your refunding money in a separate fund, do so. Cash in hand means a great deal more than profit figures on paper and will give you incentive to make even more on refunding.

CHAPTER SEVEN

Don't shop it; swap it

Now that your shopping is done and all the offers are in the mail, your refunding is finished for another week, right? Wrong. In between, you'll want to do a little swapping.

You can trade forms you can't use for ones you can. Or you can trade labels for labels, trading stamps for labels, or one kind of trading stamp or point coupon for another. Name the kind of swap you have in mind, and chances are you will find some other refunder ready to make the trade.

If you subscribe to a refunding bulletin, finding people to trade with will be the easiest part. About three-fourths of the bulletins listed in Chapter Two have classified sections in which refunders propose swaps.

FORMS

Some of the bulletin editors run a form-exchange service to expand business and give subscribers more for their money. Most editors pay rewards—such as a free issue—for information on new offers, and many refunders find they can earn all or part of their bulletin subscription costs this way. But even without rewards, it's a good policy to send information on offers to your bulletin editor, as subscribers are a main source of accurate information.

The classified section in any decent refund bulletin is normally adequate for the limited amount of trading most refunders become involved in. But if you want to do extensive swapping, you might consider subscribing to one of the half-dozen swap bulletins that list trades and swaps but do not list refund offers. There are two highly respected swap bulletins you might look over: *And More Swaps,* edited by Rose Haraburda, 233 Versailles Avenue, North Versailles, Pennsylvania 15137, sells for $.25 a copy or $2.00 a year; *Marge Hinote's Swapping Directory,* P.O. Box 630, Porterville, California 93257, sells for $.75 a copy or $3.50 a year and is the most complete listing presently available.

An even more common object of swaps is the official refund form. This is the way to get rid of forms you can't use and get those you can. Just scan your offer files, pulling out all cash and free-merchandise offer forms that don't appeal to you. Now turn to the classified section of your bulletin or to one of the swap bulletins, and scan the columns. The ad, typically placed by a refunder like yourself, will probably read "Forms, 1 for 1 plus 5, SASE, Mrs. Janice Zuk, 23 First Street, Sweet Water, Michigan." The "1 for 1" means that for every usable form you send, you will receive one in return. "Plus 5 " means that you must include five extra forms as compensation for her placing the ad. Sometimes the ad will stipulate "plus $.10," which again is to compensate the advertiser for her time. "SASE" means "self-addressed, stamped envelope," in which the swapper will return your new forms. It is understood (whether stated in the ad or not) that all correspondence between traders will include self-addressed, stamped envelopes. If you do not include one, the person receiving your forms usually feels justified in keeping them without contacting you.

Because you must include a swapping fee or extra forms and a self-addressed, stamped envelope, you would be wise to wait until you have at least twenty-five forms to swap. (This seems to be the standard swapping number.) Fewer than that just aren't worth the trouble; more will not fit into a legal-size envelope or will cost you more than $.08 for postage.

Always send the best refund forms you have (e.g. required, or "must," forms). Send a variety of forms if possible, but don't fret over duplication; no refunder will object to twenty-five identical forms if they are all good. Send long-term dates only so that you can be sure the recipient has plenty of time to use them. Typically, the person placing the ad will follow the same procedure, and you won't end up with worthless or duplicate forms. A refunder who does not send good forms soon develops a reputation among avid refunders and will find no one to trade with. Bulletin editors will even refuse to run an ad from someone noted for sending bad forms. Thus, you can be quite sure that every swap will be a profitable one.

Some trades, however, should be very carefully evaluated before you get involved in them. This is especially true of ads that offer outright sales or purchases of forms or cents-off certificates and swaps, or sale of point coupons, labels, or trading stamps. Generally, it will not be profitable to buy these items unless you cannot obtain what you need anywhere else or you have such a hoard of one kind of form or label that you can't find any other way to use it. Selling these items is not often profitable, either, unless you can deal in massive quantities.

And you should always remember that with refund forms, cents-off certificates, point coupons, and trading stamps, buying and selling at a profit can be illegal because these items are considered forms of currency. This is especially true of cash-off coupons; many bulletin editors advise that any traffic (even swaps included) in them is illegal. However, even trades on other forms are legal enough because the small fee or extra forms charged by one of the traders is a shuffling fee for handling the deal.

You will find swaps exceedingly useful for special situations that crop up in your refunding. Let's say that you have your eye on a major merchandise item, a 12-place setting of sterling silver, which takes a large number of coupons or labels that you could never accumulate on your own before the expiration date. Just place an ad in one of the refund bulletins.* The ad should clearly explain what you want (Sure-Fire coupons or Zug soap labels) and what you are willing to offer for them (labels, trading stamps, or other kinds of point coupons). You might come close to cleaning out your trash trove temporarily, but if you want the item badly enough, this is the way to get it.

COMPLETE DEALS

Trades also come in handy when you run head on into the one-per-family ruling. If a sponsor limits cash refunds or merchandise offers, then the only way to sidestep the ruling is to swap one complete deal for another. That is, you gather the labels and the required form together and

---

* In most cases, this will cost $.03 to $.05 per word.

trade the entire thing for other labels and a required form for an offer you haven't already collected on. These complete deals are normally traded on a dollar-for-dollar basis; that is, a refunder sends you three deals with a combined value of $2.25, you return as many complete deals as it takes to give the other person a $2.25 return.

The trend toward more refund offers has been juxtaposed with a trend toward limiting offers to one per family and requiring official entry forms. As these trends become more prominent, the swap will have a greater role to play in the refunder's *modus operandi.*

LABELS

Labels are another common medium of exchange among refunders. They can be bought, sold, or traded without a tinge of illegality. After all, the consumer bought the product, so the package it came in is hers to dispose of in any manner she wishes.

Although exchanging labels isn't really necessary to successful refunding, many say it's the only way to go. As one refunder put it, "I only have labels from my own groceries, but I have extras because I follow the one-per-family rule." Another said, "I have soft water, and wouldn't it be ridiculous for me to use high-sudsing detergents just to get a refund. I stick to the right product for me and swap labels for the others."

Each family, of course, uses products that others don't, so each refunder will have labels to spare.

Essentially, there are three types of label exchanges: the *potluck* exchange, which offers no choice of the kind of labels you get; the *complete deal* exchange, which means the exchange is for label-and-offer-form combinations and that all the recipient needs to do is fill in her name and address and send for the refund; and the *choice-of-return* exchange, which means that the individual offering the exchange lists everything she has available and that the other refunder can pick and choose what she wants.

Obviously, the choice-of-return method is the most useful, but it is also going to cost the label buyer more because lists must be made and details attended to. Potluck exchanges are useful, but the problem is getting labels you don't really want. The complete deal is useful only if you conscientiously follow the one-per-family ruling on some offers.

LABEL EXCHANGERS

This list of label exchangers was compiled in the summer of 1973 and should probably be useful for some time to come.

Choice of Return (exchanging complete deals, labels, and store coupons)

RADICEVIC, F., 6532 West Lindenhurst, Los Angeles, California 90048. Send $.50.

LABEL EXCHANGERS

Potluck (exchanging complete deals)

HORNBERGER, B., 670 Dori, Stowe, Pennsylvania 19464. Trades complete *cash* deals, value for value.

KELLER, J., 221 West Carrington, Oak Creek, Wisconsin 53154. Trades up to $5.00 worth complete *cash* deals, value for value, L/SASE, 10 per cent cash fee ($.20 on a $2.00 swap, $.30 on a $3.00 swap, and so forth).

MURBACH, B., Route 1, Box 14, Lyons, Ohio 43533. Trades complete *cash* deals, value for value, SASE, $.10.

REEVES, V., 9856 Crestwood, Twinsburg, Ohio 44087. Trades complete deals. No further information available.

SHREWSBURY, B., Route 1, Box 10, Basin, West Virginia 24727. Trades complete deals, value for value, SASE.

Potluck (exchanging current refundable labels)

HOLLENBAUGH, T., Route 1, Dayton, Pennsylvania 16222. Trades labels, value for value, SASE.

HORNBERGER, B., 670 Dori, Stowe, Pennsylvania 19464. Trades labels, value for value, SASE.

JAMES, L., 14B Hampton, Occidental, California 95465. Trades labels, value for value, SASE.

MARDIS, B., 111 Clay, Neillsville, Wisconsin 54456. Trades up to 10 labels, value for value, SASE, two $.08 stamps first sending only.

Offers of labels for sale usually mean potluck assortments. Some guarantee the labels will be correct parts that are usually refundable; others do not. You will profit from your investment with some assortments; others may prove a total loss.

Selling your extra labels has the same disadvantage, but in reverse: You probably cannot get more than a very small fraction of the refundable value out of them. But because you are knowledgeable about refunds, you know the true value of many labels and are not likely to be exploited. (One buyer has been in business about thirty years, buying valuable labels for perhaps ¼¢, ½¢ or 1¢ from people who are totally ignorant of the *true* value of such labels. We trust informed consumers will not fall for such lopsided deals.)

<u>Potluck</u> (buying labels)

In each case, send a SASE and ask for complete details.

BADON, H., Route 3, Box 32B, Kaplan, Louisiana 70548.

BIEWER, D., Route 2, Box 36, Milnor, North Dakota 58060.

HOLLENBAUGH, T., Route 1, Dayton, Pennsylvania 16222.

HOOK, M., Box 1549, Butler, Pennsylvania 16001.

Potluck (selling assortments of labels)
In each case, send a SASE and ask for complete details.

ALTHAUS, C., Box 73, Oak Creek, Wisconsin 53145.

BADON, H., Route 3, Box 32B, Kaplan, Louisiana 70548.

BIEWER, D., Route 2, Box 36, Milnor, North Dakota 58060.

GRUBE, J., 8812 Sproat, Oak Lawn, Illinois 60453.

HANAS, F., 344 Catalpa, Wooddale, Illinois 60191.

KAZ, M., 22111 DeLaOsa, Woodland Hills, California 91364.

KRAUSE, D., Route 4, Mitchell, South Dakota 57301.

PITCOCK, N., 76 Ruth, Pontiac, Michigan 48053.

RADICEVIC, F., 6532 West Lindenhurst, Los Angeles, California 90048.

REFUND-FORM EXCHANGERS

The following list will give you a head start in swaps. Each person listed has expressed the intention to make exchanges throughout 1973. Beyond the end of the year many may drop out, so for courtesy's sake, send a self-addressed, stamped envelope if you correspond with them.

ADAMS, K., Route 2, Box 97, Delphos, Kansas 67436. Send 25 blanks, SASE (25).*

AMICK, J., Route 3, Bedford, Indiana 47421. Send 20 blanks, SASE, 1 current refundable label (20).

BADON, T., Route 3, Box 32B, Kaplan, Louisiana 70548. Send up to 30 blanks, SASE, $.08 stamp (1 for 1).

BAIRD, J., Box 74, Loschton, Georgia 30548. Send up to 20 blanks, SASE, current refundable label (1 for 1).

BARTLETT, R., 86 Highland Avenue, Wallingford, Connecticut 06492. Send up to 25 blanks, SASE, $.10 (1 for 1).

BAUMANN, E., 476 Germantown, Rt. 2, Butler, New Jersey 07405. Send 20 blanks, SASE (1 for 1).

BEAR, M., 15 Hodgdon, W. Roxbury, Massachusetts 02132. Send 30 *different* blanks, SASE, $.10 (25).

BEATTY, L., 1433 Elliott, Verona, Pennsylvania 15147. Send up to 30 blanks, SASE (1 for 1).

---

* The number in parentheses indicates how many forms you will get in return.

REFUND-FORM EXCHANGERS

BELL, R., 470 Forest Hill, Youngstown, Ohio 44515. Send up to 30 blanks, SASE, $.10 (1 for 1).

BENSON, J., 702 N. Wilson, Rice Lake, Wisconsin 54868. Send up to 30 blanks, SASE, $.15 *or* two loose $.08 stamps *or* 3 current refundable labels (1 for 1).

BIEWER, D., Rt. 2, Box 36, Milnor, North Dakota 58060. Send up to 30 blanks, SASE (1 for 1).

BLACKWELL, J., 210 Hilltop, Morganton, North Carolina 28655. Send 20 blanks, SASE, $.08 stamp (20).

BOND, F., 300 Mt. View, Westminster, South Carolina 29693. Send 25 blanks, SASE (25).

BOUCKAERT, D., 3810 E. McGilvra, Seattle, Washington 98112. Send up to 30 blanks, SASE (1 for 1).

BRASSARD, J., 2710 19th Avenue, N. Texas City, Texas 77590. Send up to 20 blanks, SASE (1 for 1).

BRUNNER, H., 3859 N. 70th, Milwaukee, Wisconsin 53216. Send 30 blanks, SASE, $.25 (45).

CALABRIA, A., 16 Herbert, Englishtown, New Jersey 07726. Send up to 30 blanks, SASE (1 for 1).

CARROLL, D., Rt. 1, Box 48-B, Ellwood City, Pennsylvania 16117. Send up to 30 blanks, SASE, $.25 (1 for 1).

CLICK, G., 508 Lincoln, Clarksville, Indiana 47130. Send 30 blanks, SASE, $.10 (30).

COLE, P., 1169 Zurich, San Jose, California 96132. Send up to 25 blanks, SASE (1 for 1).

CONNELLY, M., Rt. 4, Box 108, Irwin, Pennsylvania 15642. Send 15 blanks, SASE (15).

CONNERTON, F., 40 Evergreen, Lincoln Park, New Jersey 07035. Send 25 blanks, SASE (25).

COOPER, P., 601 S. Randall #B, Elk City, Oklahoma 73644. Send 25 blanks, SASE (25).

CORLEY, G., Rt. 4, Batesville, Mississippi 38606. Send up to 25 blanks, SASE (1 for 1).

CUNDY, J., 625 Johanna, Sunnyvale, California 94086. Send 20 blanks, SASE, current refundable label (20).

D'ANTICO, B., 69 Mayfield, Cranston, Rhode Island 02920. Send 30 blanks, SASE (30).

DANIELS, P., 13460 Cloverlawn, Sterling Hts., Michigan 48077. Send 25 blanks, SASE (25).

DEARDORFF, M., 5735 Roswell N.E., Apt. D-7, Atlanta, Georgia 30342. Send up to 30 blanks, SASE (1 for 1).

DEMCHAK, L., Box 73, Crucible, Pennsylvania 15325. Send up to 30 blanks, SASE (1 for 1).

REFUND-FORM EXCHANGERS

DETIG, M., 1723 Hollyrood, Pittsburgh, Pennsylvania 15227. Send up to 25 blanks, SASE, current refundable label (1 for 1).

DOBIES, N., 6339 Fellrath, Taylor, Michigan 48180. Send 25 blanks, SASE, 2 Stokely-Van Camp labels (35).

DREWS, B., 13435 S. Stephen, Palos Park, Illinois 60464. Send up to 30 blanks, SASE (1 for 1).

FEENEY, H., 2317 Ramsey, New Orleans, Louisiana 70114. Send 25 blanks, SASE (1 for 1).

FETTERLY, C., Rt. 1, Oconto Falls, Wisconsin 54154. Send up to 25 blanks, SASE, current refundable label (1 for 1).

FISHER, C., Rt. 2, Bruce, Mississippi 38915. Send up to 25 blanks, SASE (1 for 1).

FISLER, M., 1312 Groveland, Venice, Florida 33595. Send up to 20 blanks, SASE (1 for 1).

FLECKENSTEIN, F., 7621 Chillicothe, Mentor, Ohio 44060. Send 20 blanks, SASE, two loose $.08 stamps (25).

FOSTER, T., 15103 Carol Chase, Missouri City, Texas 77459. Send up to 15 blanks, SASE (1 for 1).

FRANS, R., 4514 Madison, Omaha, Nebraska 68117. Send up to 30 blanks, SASE, $.10 (1 for 1).

GAUSE, M., Rt. 1, Box 475, Yakima, Washington 98901. Send up to 20 blanks, SASE (1 for 1).

GILTNER, R., 2035 McAdams, Dallas, Texas 75224. Send 20 to 30 blanks, SASE, $.25 (30 to 45).

GORNEY, R., 145 Duerstein, Buffalo, New York 14210. Send up to 30 blanks, SASE (1 for 1).

GOSSE, B., 10803 Candlewood, Houston, Texas 77042. Send up to 30 blanks, SASE, $.08 loose stamp (1 for 1).

GRUBE, J., 8812 Sproat, Oak Lawn, Illinois 60453. Send up to 30 blanks, SASE, 1 current refundable label (1 for 1).

GRYN, J., 17167 Lamont, Detroit, Michigan 48212. Send 30 blanks, SASE, $.10 (25).

GUERRIERO, M., 26412 Warrington, Dearborn Hts., Michigan 48127. Send 30 blanks, SASE, current refundable label (30).

HANAS, F., 344 Catalpa, Wooddale, Illinois 60191. Send up to 30 blanks, SASE (1 for 1).

HANSON, W., 22214 Navaho, Sauk Village, Illinois 60411. Send 25 blanks, SASE (25).

HASTE, E., 25 Elmgrove, Providence, Rhode Island 02906. Send up to 25 blanks, SASE (1 for 1).

HEIDAMI, P., 7261 Shore, Apt. 2-R, Brooklyn, New York 11209. Send up to 50 *different* blanks (none for gifts), SASE, two loose $.08 stamps (1 for 1).

REFUND-FORM EXCHANGERS

HEIM, D., Rt. G3, Luxemburg, Wisconsin 54217. Send up to 30 blanks, SASE (1 for 1).

HENDERSON, C., 22 Withee, Madison, Maine 04950. Send up to 30 blanks, SASE (1 for 1).

HOLLENBAUGH, T., Rt. 1, Dayton, Pennsylvania 16222. Send 30 blanks, SASE (30).

HOLLOWOOD, J., 1007 Aetna, Connellsville, Pennsylvania 15425. Send up to 30 blanks, SASE, $.08 loose stamp (1 for 1).

HOOK, M., Box 1549, Butler, Pennsylvania 16001. Send up to 30 blanks, SASE, $.10 (1 for 1).

HORNBERGER, B., 670 Dori, Stowe, Pennsylvania 19464. Send up to 30 blanks, SASE, 1 current refundable label (1 for 1).

HUMPHREY, E., 2105 E. "L," Omaha, Nebraska 68110. Send 30 blanks, SASE, 1 current refundable label (1 for 1).

IVERSON, R., 8552 Tyler N.E., Minneapolis, Minnesota 55434. Send up to 35 blanks, SASE (1 for 1).

JAMES, L., 14B Hampton, Occidental, California 95465. Send up to 30 blanks, SASE (1 for 1 plus bonus).

JOHNSON, B., Rt. 1, Emporia, Kansas 66801. Send 20 blanks, SASE (20).

JOHNSON, J., Fisher, Conneautville, Pennsylvania 16406. Send up to 30 *must* blanks, SASE (1 for 1).

JOHNSON, M., Rt. 1, Box 169, Blissfield, Michigan 49228. Send 25 blanks, SASE, $.08 loose stamp (25).

JOHNSTON, J., 9628 W. Concordia, Milwaukee, Wisconsin 53222. Send up to 30 blanks, SASE, $.10 (1 for 1).

KACHURIK, S., 2146 W. Armitage, Chicago, Illinois 60647. Send 30 blanks, SASE, 1 current refundable label (30).

KAYE, L., P.O. Box 8044, Milwaukee, Wisconsin 53223. Send 30 blanks, SASE, $.25 (35 *cash* offers).

KAZ, M., 22111 DeLaOsa, Woodland Hills, California 91364. Send 25 blanks, SASE (25).

KINDLE, D., 2939 10th, R. Moline, Illinois 61244. Send 30 blanks, SASE, $.25 (30).

KLINE, P., 4031 Greenwood, New Kensington, Pennsylvania 15068. Send 25 blanks, SASE (25).

KNOLL, R., 156 St. James, Webster, New York 14580. Send 20 to 30 blanks, SASE (1 for 1).

KWOCK, B., 1459 Kaumoli, Pearl City, Hawaii 96782. Send up to 30 blanks, SASE (1 for 1).

LAPLANTE, L., 31538 Madison, Madison Hts., Michigan 48071. Send 25 blanks, SASE (25).

LAWRENCE, D., Rt. 1, Fountain City,

Indiana 47341. Send up to 30 blanks, SASE (1 for 1).

LENZINI, R., 831 Walnut, Macon, Missouri 63552. Send up to 30 blanks, SASE (1 for 1).

LISIEWICZ, E., 2614 Weisman, Wheaton, Maryland 20902. Send up to 30 blanks, SASE, $.25 (1 for 1).

LYONS, W., 6828 Chew, Philadelphia, Pennsylvania 19119. Send 15 blanks, SASE, $.25 (30).

MACKEY, H., 1507 Banmoor, Troy, Michigan 48084. Send up to 30 blanks, SASE (1 for 1).

MADALINSKI, M., 705 S. Braintree, Schaumburg, Illinois 60172. Send 25 blanks, SASE, $.10 (25).

MAHLE, M., Fultonham, Ohio 43738. Send up to 30 blanks, SASE, $.15 (1 for 1).

MARDIS, B., 111 Clay, Neillsville, Wisconsin 54456. Send up to 25 blanks, SASE, two loose $.08 stamps first time only (1 for 1).

MARSH, P., 1470 Village Green, Adrian, Michigan 49221. Send up to 30 blanks, SASE, 1 current refundable label (1 for 1).

MARTENS, H., Emmet, Nebraska 68734. Send 20 blanks, SASE (20).

MATOUSEK, H., Box 32, Unionville, Michigan 48767. Send 20 *cash* blanks, SASE (20).

MCCLAIN, P., P.O. Box G, Williamsburg, Indiana 47393. Send up to 50 blanks, SASE (1 for 1).

MELANO, J., 4123 E. Croydon, Camarillo, California 93010. Send up to 40 blanks, SASE (1 for 1).

METZ, A., Lacona, Iowa 50139. Send up to 30 blanks, SASE (1 for 1).

MILLER, G., 1446 Sleepy Hollow, Paradise, California 95969. Send up to 30 blanks, SASE (1 for 1).

MILNER, K., Rt. 1, Larsen, Wisconsin 54947. Send 30 blanks, SASE, $.10 (30).

MINARICK, A., 608 Fairview, Pottsville, Pennsylvania 17901. Send up to 30 blanks, SASE (1 for 1).

MISCOVICH, R., 17066 Wausau, South Holland, Illinois 60473. Send 30 blanks, SASE, $.15 (30).

MOELL, J., 113 N. Rauthland, Wapakoneta, Ohio 45895. Send 15 blanks, SASE (20).

MURBACH, B., Rt. 1, Box 14, Lyons, Ohio 43533. Send 20 *must* blanks, SASE, $.10 (20 *must*).

NELSON, B., Oldfield, Missouri 65720. Send 30 blanks, SASE, $.10 (30).

NITROY, A., 3138 Street, Warrington, Pennsylvania 18976. Send up to 25 blanks, SASE (1 for 1).

REFUND-FORM EXCHANGERS

NORFLEET, K., 336 Flossmoor, Waukegan, Illinois 60085. Send up to 30 blanks, SASE (1 for 1).

OWENS, J., 12 Bonnie, New Hartford, New York 13413. Send up to 30 blanks, SASE (1 for 1).

PASTERNAK, J., 6331 Grandview, Erie, Michigan 48133. Send up to 30 blanks, SASE (1 for 1).

PESSES, L., 1510 Brady, Davenport, Iowa 52803. Send up to 35 blanks, SASE, $.20 (1 for 1).

PETERSON, J., 1301 Orchard, Racine, Wisconsin 53405. Send 20 blanks, SASE (20).

PITCOCK, N., 76 Ruth, Pontiac, Michigan 48053. Send 20 blanks, SASE, current refundable label (20).

PROCHASKA, G., Box 133, Winnetoon, Nebraska 68789. Send 30 blanks, SASE, $.10 (30).

PRYOR, S., 438 Ralstin, Wichita, Kansas 67209. Send up to 30 blanks, SASE, 25 Gift Star coupons *or* trading stamps (1 for 1).

RADICEVIC, F., 6532 W. Lindenhurst, Los Angeles, California 90048. Send 30 blanks, SASE, $.15 (30).

REEVES, V., 9856 Crestwood, Twinsburg, Ohio 44087. Send up to 30 blanks, SASE, $.10 (1 for 1).

REINHOLD, M., 104 Somerset, Valparaiso, Indiana 46383. Send 20 blanks, SASE, two $.08 stamps (20).

RESSLER, J., 2010 W. Chestnut, Cadillac, Michigan 49601. Send up to 30 blanks, SASE (1 for 1).

RILEY, D., 1220 W. Copper, Hobbs, New Mexico 88240. Send 30 blanks, SASE, $.20 (25).

RYAN, S., 942 Gulf, Attica, New York 14011. Send up to 40 blanks, SASE (1 for 1).

SCADDEN, I., 4517 Julivan S.E., Grand Rapids, Michigan 49508. Send 30 blanks, SASE, $.25 (35).

SCHEIDLER, G., 150 Cherry, Hellertown, Pennsylvania 18055. Send 25 blanks, SASE (25).

SCHIEVELBEIN, B., Rt. 3, Box 363, Seguin, Texas 78155. Send 25 blanks, SASE, current refundable label (30).

SCHLEGEL, M., 2941 225th St., Sauk Village, Illinois 60411. Send 20 blanks, SASE (1 for 1).

SCHULKEY, M., 221 Pacific, Elkhorn, Nebraska 68022. Send 20 blanks, SASE (20).

SCHWARTZ, N., Rt. 2, Box 109, Waterville, Minnesota 56096. Send 30 blanks, SASE (30).

SCOTT, C., 637 Reco, Minneapolis, Minnesota 55432. Send 25 blanks, SASE, $.10 (30).

REFUND-FORM EXCHANGERS

SELANDER, B., Rt. 1, Gowrie, Iowa 50543. Send 20 blanks (none for gifts), SASE (20).

SHANE, J., 1623 H-6 Judie, Lancaster, Pennsylvania 17603. Send 20 blanks, SASE, $.10 (25).

SHAPIRO, L., 6471 S.W. 22d, Miami, Florida 33155. Send 30 blanks, SASE, $.25 (40).

SHINN, M., 945 Virgil, Gas City, Indiana 46933. Send 30 blanks, SASE (30).

SHREWSBURY, B., Rt. 1, Box 10, Basin, West Virginia 24727. Send up to 30 blanks, SASE (1 for 1).

SMILEY, I., 37739 Bankside, Palm Springs, California 92262. Send 25 blanks, SASE (25).

SMITH, J., 3209 Washington, Erie, Pennsylvania 16508. Send 20 blanks, SASE (20).

SNAIR, G., 277 N. Marcello, Thousand Oaks, California 91360. Send 15 blanks, SASE, 1 current refundable label (20).

SORENSON, A., 109 E. Hill, Lead, South Dakota 57754. Send 15 blanks, SASE (15).

SPIVEY, L., 2110 E. Clay, Indianapolis, Indiana 46205. Send 20 blanks, SASE, $.10 (20).

STARK, G., 2804 Lutz, Mansfield, Ohio 44903. Send 30 blanks, SASE, $.10 (30).

STOKES, P., 381 Montpelier, Forsyth, Georgia 31029. Send 25 blanks, SASE,

$.10 *or* $.08 loose stamp *or* current refundable label (25).

TADYSAK, J., 1318 S. 76th, W. Allis, Wisconsin 53214. Send 20 blanks, SASE (20).

TAMEL, J., 5942 Seneca, Hales Corners, Wisconsin 53130. Send 30 blanks, SASE, $.25 (35).

TAYLOR, M., Cedarville, Millville, New Jersey 08332. Send 25 blanks, SASE, $.20 (25).

TREGO, V., P.O. Box 273, Atascadero, California 93422. Send 25 blanks, SASE (25).

USZCIENSKI, E., 314 Washington, Carpentersville, Illinois 60110. Send 30 blanks (15 *must* included), SASE, $.25 (30, 10 *must* included).

WHERRY, M., 9380 85th St., Apt. C, Rock Island, Illinois 61201. Send 30 blanks, SASE, $.25 (30).

CHAPTER EIGHT

Is there a gambler in the house?

Normally, refunders are the pragmatic sort; they invest time in clipping coupons and mailing labels and in turn are assured of direct rewards in hard cash or merchandise. But to many, this businesslike undertaking can sometimes get a trifle dull. So to avoid the doldrums and take a shot at grander prizes than conventional couponing can offer, lots of refunders go in for box-top contests.

Box-top contests can net participants tens of thousands of dollars in prize money and some rather spectacular goods, such as new cars, color TVs, sailboats, riding lawn mowers, and grand pianos. On the other hand, your best contest efforts may not earn you the price of a single postage stamp. It's a gamble. For this reason, many refunders refuse to get involved in contesting. They feel that in refunding, time is money and that every moment invested in such speculative activities is money which could have been earned with an equivalent amount of time spent on regular refund offers.

But there *are* good reasons to gamble on contests. First of all, box-top contestants stand a far greater chance of winning than Irish sweepstakes or state lottery contestants. Better yet, box-top contestants needn't risk anything more than a stamp and an envelope to have a chance at winning. Typically, prizes are donated by merchants who want product exposure, so the rewards can be broader than they are in a paid drawing or lottery. And because refunders are already set up to handle mailings and to fill out entry forms correctly (incorrectly filled-out forms are the biggest disqualifier in contests), they've got a decided advantage in competing.

Granted your odds of winning are slim, but they're much better if you enter than if you don't. Entering is inexpensive. Sponsors would *like* to require that entrants send a box top or label as a proof of purchase of their product in order to enter a contest, but they can't because to do so would be to run an illegal lottery (even in states that now have their own legal lotteries). So they attempt to circumvent the law by asking for one of a number of facsimiles of the product label. Because a sponsor feels cheated when you send in a facsimile with your entry instead of a box top, he will often look it over carefully, seeking a reason to disqualify you. One trick is to confuse the entrant with verbiage. For example, a "reasonable facsimile" means you are to trace or draw a duplicate of the required label. A sloppy sketch or a duplicating-machine copy will be rejected. Now if they ask for "block letters" of the product name, they don't want it to look like the original. What they want, simply, is printing, for example, SOAPY DETERGENT. Sometimes sponsors request a facsimile "in writing," which means you're to write it in longhand. (In all cases, plain paper or a three-by-five-inch card should suffice.) It's generally easier to send in the label than to play the reasonable-facsimile game, but if you do enter with a facsimile, be assured they can't discriminate against your entry. If you're picked, you win, or the federal government will ask why you didn't.

TYPES OF CONTESTS

Essentially, there are three types of contests to consider: *skill contests,* in which your ability or knowledge of a subject is needed; *sweepstakes,* which are essentially no more than drawings; and the nearly defunct *preselected-winner contests,* which are quickly recognized by the catch phrase "You may have already won."

Skill contests are the least common because sponsors find it far too expensive to judge or at least evaluate all entries. Yet they offer the best odds of winning. Skill and effort are required, and the result is that fewer people enter the contest. To the sponsor, fewer contestants mean less exposure for the product. But it also means you've got an increased probability of taking a prize. Niles Eggleston, who has been entering contests since the early 1930s and has won thousands of prizes over the years, suggests that the odds can be made still better if the contestant will stick to contests involving his or her specialities (e.g., recipe contests such as the $100,000 Pillsbury contest or crossword puzzle contests).

In the sweepstakes contest, all you must do is fill in an entry form, attach a label or box top (or a reasonable facsimile of a label) to it, and mail it in. Your entry will go into the barrel with all the others waiting to be drawn when the contest closes. Entries in this form of contest easily surpass 1 million with the least advertising imaginable, so your chance of winning a prize is slight compared with skill competition.

You can increase your chances by entering frequently. Few of these sponsors specify one entry per family, and as in the case of refund offers, the few companies that try to limit entrants do not go to the expense of searching for duplicates. If you decide to enter more than once, spread your mailings over the entire length of the contest. Send only one entry per envelope. Envelopes often are not opened until after the drawing, so four entries in one container will have the same chance of being drawn as one entry. And it only stands to reason that your chances are better in a drawing with many small prizes rather than one big prize.

It seems that when it comes to the actual drawings, justice is seldom blind. Contest veterans use several gimmicks to enhance their luck in the draw. Usually a secretary is elected to dig into the barrel and pull out the winners. To catch her attention and therefore her draw, entrants can use oversized, eye-catching envelopes. Colored envelopes and envelopes with hand-drawn illustrations are also used successfully. Instead of neatly printing or typing their addresses on the envelopes, many use large writing done in colored ink or with a felt-tip pen. And just in case the hand of fate is digging deep into the barrel, envelopes made of heavier-than-normal paper stock will attract sensitive fingers.

With the help of these devices, hundreds of professional contestants are gathering up the goodies. Bill Danch of Hollywood, California, to name just one, has received more than 2,000 prizes (ranging from a two-week trip to the Bahamas to a color TV) over a ten-year period, and entering contests is only an infrequent hobby with him. In one contest alone, Bill won eleven cameras (which proves that the one-prize-per-family rule is ineffectual in practice).

IS THERE A GAMBLER IN THE HOUSE?

Although these sweepstakes or drawings are admittedly gambling, they're appreciably less of a gamble than those that you have to pay to enter, such as the new state lotteries or race track betting. Why? Simply because the box-top sweepstakes is a self-liquidating advertisement in which the sponsor (unlike an oddsmaker) does not rake off profits. The entire cost, including prizes, is born by the sponsor, who hopes to gain your continued patronage after the thrill of competing is past.

Preselected-winner drawings constitute the shadiest of all advertising promotions and have received a lot of attention in recent years. It is this form of contest that has given all advertising contests a black eye and reduced the number of contest promotions significantly. (But don't worry, there are still hundreds of contests around.) The basic idea is that the winning numbers have already been picked and then prenumbered entry blanks are given out. To find out if you've won or not, you must go into the sponsors' store or gas station and compare your number to a master list. Or, in the case of magazine sponsors, you must send in a subscription envelope (but you don't have to subscribe).

The catch is that a sponsor can offer $1 million in prizes knowing full well that less than 5 per cent of the prizes will ever be given out. They're playing the odds that say if you mail out 1,000 forms, your return rate will normally be no more than 5 per cent (just 50) and typically less than

2 per cent (20). The sponsor takes no chances with such a contest; whereas with sweepstakes, for example, if he offers 1,000 prizes and gets only 1,000 entries, then everyone gets a prize.

FTC investigations revealed some startling figures on these contests. Four million entry forms were sent out by Union Carbide in a $50,000 contest, yet not a penny was ever paid out in prizes. Clairol offered twenty-five new cars as prizes and gave out none of them. Other companies investigated paid out from nothing to 2.7 per cent of the total prize money. In short, the odds were all in the advertisers' favor.

The FTC came down hard on these deceptive practices. They ordered that all future contests must advertise the individual's odds of winning, the area the contest is to cover, and the precise closing dates. In response, nearly all the preselected-winner contests disappeared. The few sponsors that remained, Reader's Digest being the largest, cleaned up their contest advertising to conform with the FTC's rulings.

Preselected-winner contests have not gotten all the attention. A number of skill contests have also been disputed. Coca-Cola, for example, was recently attacked by the FTC for its Big Name Bingo contest, in which the questions to be answered were considered ambiguous. No indication was made on the entry blank or in advertising the contest that more than one answer per question was needed, and yet only those

IS THERE A GAMBLER IN THE HOUSE?

who gave multiple answers won. The FTC has demanded that the company pay out more than $200 million to entrants who should rightfully have won under the printed rules. Obviously, Coca-Cola and Glendenning Corporation, which ran the contest, will fight this decision in court for years to come.

Sponsors appear to take far more liberties with their ethics when it comes to operating contests than they have with refund offers. But as long as the FTC and other federal watchdog agencies are in business, you can enter with some assurance that a sponsoring company that tries to cheat you may be taking a bigger chance than its contestants.

If you want to try your luck, you might look into one of the following contest bulletins:

CONTEST ANNOUNCEMENTS, Eggleston Enterprises, 1 South Main Street, Milford, New York 13807, $.35 per copy, $3.48 annually.

GENERAL CONTEST BULLETIN, 1609 East 5th Street, Duluth, Minnesota 55812, $.25 per copy, $2.50 annually.

CONTEST WORKSHEET, Box 4027, Dallas, Texas 75208, $.50 per copy, $5.00 annually.

SHEPHERD SCHOOL, P.O. Box 366, Willingboro, New Jersey 08046, $.50 per copy, $4.25 for 11 issues (published weekly).

CHAPTER NINE

Charity, sweet charity

Try as we may to resist, virtually all of us who have families are eventually drawn into the community of family organizations. Churches, Ys, civic leagues, PTAs, fraternal organizations, social clubs, and quasi-professional groups make demands on our time and talents, and we soon find ourselves sharing the aspirations and frustrations of the groups. Each of us can contribute our own unique talents to help a group achieve its goals. Refunders can contribute their special talent: making money. After all, money is one commodity organizations always seem to need.

CASH REFUNDS

Your group can earn money through one or more of the many channels open to refunders. The most obvious, of course, is cash refunding. The fund-raising chairwoman should subscribe to a refund bulletin. She picks out one or two particularly worthwhile offers that do not require more than one or two labels each. Then at the regular group meeting, the chairwoman announces the offers to be obtained and asks that all members try to bring the required labels to the next regularly scheduled meeting. She also asks each person to bring a three-by-five-inch card on which she has printed her name and address. When the labels and addresses come in, the fund-raising committee sends them out in the names of the members who supplied the labels. When the money comes to the member's home, she can bring it to the meeting, along with more labels for the next announced offer. It's a good idea to distribute general lists of labels to be saved so that members can help to build a group trash trove.

As a source of working capital, this method surely beats ice cream socials and cookie sales, and it has the distinct advantage of continuing week after week. Most manufacturers have no objection to this charitable effort; after all, people are buying and using the product. But a few manufacturers object strenuously on the grounds that purchases by group members just for the purpose of a refund do not build loyal customers. Others object because they've been stung. The classic example occurred in 1960 when a company offered to send "one dollar to your favorite charity" for six of their tuna fish can labels. An enterprising religious organization ordered 144,000 cans of fish and asked that the refund be sent to themselves. This company can give you $24,000 worth of reasons why they do not like to get involved with fund-raising campaigns.

You can tell how a company feels about this issue by reading the refund-offer instructions. If they specify "one to a family or *group*," no doubt the company doesn't want their cash refunds supporting your charity. Technically, if each member of a group sends in the offer in her own name and then donates her refund money to the group, you could say that the one-refund-per-family-or-group rule was being honored. Furthermore, what company could or would object to how the individual donates his or her refund money? Actually, this is the best method for group refunding because most clearinghouses are set up to process only those refunds that come in and go out one to an envelope.

LABELS AND BOX TOPS

Another way to make money for your organization is by selling labels or box tops. You will notice in your refund bulletin occasional ads from people who make a business of buying and selling labels. As you have learned, it is not profitable for the individual refunder to sell a few labels to such dealers, but large shipments of labels from a group make these one-shot sales profitable.

MERCHANDISE

Yet another way of building group funds is to hold a bazaar using prizes supplied through merchandise-refund offers. With at least six months of planning to assure enough prizes for the different booths, a bazaar can yield a 100 per cent profit. As in the case of the cash-refund approach, group members are assigned a free-merchandise offer to send for and then donate to the group.

GROUP PLANS

Perhaps the most popular of all the various group approaches is the General Mills Betty Crocker club program. Under this plan, group members collect Betty Crocker coupons and redeem them for some major item such as an organ for a church, a school bus, or diagnostic machines for a local hospital. Groups may register with General Mills and request approval for their project. The cash-redemption rate on approved projects is ½¢ per coupon.

The efforts of one small women's club in North Plainfield, New Jersey, illustrate how easy a coupon drive can be. In less than six months, they collected 60,000 coupons for a $3,000 kidney machine. These group redemptions of Betty Crocker coupons account for one-third of all coupons redeemed by General Mills.

Companies like General Mills are delighted to work with you and to do all they can to be of assistance—within the bounds of good business. This is especially true of point-coupon and trading-stamp companies; virtually all have special programs established for groups. (See Chapter Four for a list of these companies.)

If you would like your group to take advantage of a company offer, write to the customer relations or public relations department of that company. Explain your group goals, and ask politely for their assistance. Most of them will either agree to help or politely tell you to take your charity elsewhere. Either way, you haven't lost anything but a stamp.

CHAPTER TEN

Free for all

No word in the American language has been more thoroughly abused and misused than *free*. Typically, when admen say something is "absolutely free" in big bold print, it is followed by entry-requirement lines in type small enough to make an eagle squint. Refunding offers are frequently described as "free money" or "free merchandise" obtained just by sending in so many box tops and perhaps some loose change. Small wonder, then, that most of us don't raise an eyebrow when offered a valuable item free. We wait for the catch.

But believe it or not, there are people out there giving away something for nothing. *Freebies*, as refunders call them, are items of some worth given away by hundreds of manufacturers, trade associations, and government agencies just for the asking. Typical freebies include recipe booklets, free merchandise samples, redecorating ideas, travel information and maps, and even free magazine subscriptions.

Except in the case of government literature, which is obviously paid for with your tax dollars, most of these freebies are structured as subtle promotions of product lines or entire industries. This is the soft sell at its best because the public gets something more than blarney in the process.

Like refund offers, freebie offers are advertised in magazines and newspapers, on product packages, and in grocery stores. And as in refunding, there are several booklets or bulletins that list from a few to a few hundred freebies. Here are some of these sources of freebie offers:

DOLLAR BARGAINS, P.O. Box 1225, Newark, New Jersey 07101.

Send $1.00 for a sixty-four-page freebies book *1001 Things Free*. This seems to be a well-researched booklet.

FREE, Department TE, P.O. Box 3434, Seminole, Florida 33542.

Send $3.23 (money-back guarantee) for subscription (length not mentioned) to bimonthly newsletter listing free offers.

SEWING BOOK OFFER, 17th Floor, 225 Park Avenue South, New York, New York 10003.

Send $.25 for *501 Valuable Things Free*.

FREE GIFTS, Department WD7, Box 5548, Inglewood, California 90310.

Send $1.00 for one-page list of 75 freebie items.

FREE GIFTS, P.O. Box 981, FDR Station, New York, New York 10022.

Send $1.00 for list of over 100 freebie items.

MAIL ORDER CATALOG DIRECTORY, Box 305, Plymouth Meeting, Pennsylvania 19462.

Price (if any) unknown. Lists catalogs available free (or for a small handling charge).

GIVEAWAYS, 520 North Greece Road, Hilton, New York 14468.

Send $.40 for mimeographed list of about 40 freebie items.

HOW TO SEND FOR FREEBIES

Make requests for freebies on postcards, unless an offer requires a self-addressed, stamped envelope. Postcard requests save companies endless time in opening envelopes and reading long request letters on many different sizes of paper. If a self-addressed, stamped envelope is asked for, *be sure you enclose one.* It's always best to provide a No. 10 business-size envelope (9½ by 4 inches). Canadian residents should enclose postage money when providing a return envelope or place a U.S. stamp on it. (Do not use Canadian stamps.)

Make your request brief, and make it clear. Be sure you write your name and address very clearly, and use your zip code. If you have printed address labels, use them. Don't send for items you really can't use or information you are not truly interested in. And don't forget to be courteous in your request letters and express appreciation to the sponsor.

CHAPTER ELEVEN

The graduation lecture

Before you're booted out from under the sheltered pages of this book and into the stark realities of the refunding world, there are several thoughts you would do well to carry with you which we will call the Nine Commandments of Refunding.

1. All that glitters isn't a bargain. Some products with attractive cash refunds attached are not worth the effort. Always comparison shop to make sure the product is not so overpriced that you can't realize a profit by sending for the rebate. This is especially applicable to the convenience foods such as complete frozen dinners or exotic meat dishes. Convenience foods are just that, a convenience; and you normally pay an exorbitant price for the advantage of not preparing the meal yourself. For two- and three-member families, these convenience foods often are cheaper than doing it yourself; for larger families, they seldom are. Calculate how much you will save by purchasing the item with the cash refund or cents-off certificate before you buy.

2. Little offers aren't much. With the postal rates at $.08 and going up to $.10 in January, 1974, it may not pay you to bother with $.15 and $.25 cash-refund offers. Most of the companies realize this and have gone to bigger refunds of $1.00, $2.00, or $3.00. But just as there are some companies that haven't raised their hourly wages since World War II, there are companies that still haven't realized that inflation has come to the American home. You may wish to set yourself an arbitrary minimum of $.50 offers and only break it when you've got nothing better to do. However, if you're going to use the products anyway, a $.25 refund, less an $.08 stamp, still nets a 68 per cent profit (but only a $.17 return). You must ask yourself how much your time is worth.

3. Time is money. Some aspects of refunding are notable only for tediousness, so use every shortcut method you can conjure up to keep these duties to a minimum. Using a rubber stamp or gummed address labels is one time-saving trick; using prestamped envelopes is another. You will no doubt discover many more such tricks as you become more involved in refunding.

4. Be your own final inspector. Just before you seal that envelope and rush off another offer, check to be positive everything is in order. Your address and the address of the company should be legibly marked on the envelope. Inside the envelope you should have the required labels; count them again. You should also enclose a card or slip of paper three by five inches or larger on which you have printed your name and address and a line of explanation of the offer ("$1.00 for five 10-ounce soup can labels"). If an official entry blank is required, be sure it is filled out and enclosed. And check the stamp on the envelope one last time. This final inspection will save you refunding dollars in the long run.

5. Meticulousness matters. Be organized. Never send a refund offer unless you have logged it in your book. Unless you keep accurate records, you'll have no way of knowing whether you are taking advantage of refunding or it is taking advantage of you.

6. Don't freak out on refunds. A popular joke among refunders is about the woman who is showing a friend all the furniture and housewares she bought just by taking advantage of one dried-beans offer.

"All the furniture in this house was paid for by that cash offer," the lady boasted.

"That's nice," the guest said, "but you've only shown me two rooms. What about the other rooms?"

"Oh, those," the lady answered. "I can't show you those because they're filled with beans."

To many overzealous refunders, there is more truth than humor in this joke. Stocking up on a product because it offers a spectacular refund at the moment is fine if it doesn't get out of hand. The rule of thumb should be to stay within your budget at all times. And do *not* buy products you do not need, cannot use, or will not use because of finicky appetites.

7. Never call yourself a "professional" refunder. Although most companies will grant you a cash or merchandise refund even if they feel you are on the border of being a professional refunder, some companies won't. Refunds, they say, are to introduce potentially loyal customers to a product. Because refunders skip from one bargain offer to another, they will never be dedicated customers who will not trade a favorite brand for twice as much of brand X. The majority of the advertising men and sponsoring companies realize that refunders are simply housewives with an above-average aptitude for getting their money's worth. But there are enough of the disgruntled types around for you to be cautious.

8. Ethics buy insurance. More and more companies are turning to cash- and merchandise-refund offers as a practical advertising medium. If this trend is to continue, it will be because refunders learn that ethics pay. Unscrupulous refunders have given sponsors more than a fair share of headaches, and when the number of problems reaches the point of diminishing returns, refund offers will be terminated. It will be a *few* who ruin a good thing for many honest ones.

Storekeepers regularly report that women tear off box tops, endseals, and even jar lids from shelf merchandise just to get refunds. This amounts to petty theft and should be punished accordingly. More common are the refunders who grab every offer blank from a display pad so that they can profiteer by selling the forms to fellow refunders through refund bulletins. This gives the refunders and the bulletins a black eye with companies. Likewise, sending in fifty refund requests on an offer that states "limited one to a family" is blatant dishonesty. Don't be greedy; there are more than enough offers to go around.

9. Join the club. Refunders are a closely knit group. They eventually become pen pals through the reams of correspondence involved in offer swaps and tip sharing. Many refunders place this fellowship high on their list of refunding rewards. This is especially true of shut-ins, retirees, and women who can't often get out of the house because they have large families. One sixty-five-year-old woman wrote to tell us about refunding. She spent four pages describing all the wonderful women she had met through her correspondence, and only in the last sentence of her letter did she get around to mentioning the profits she had received. Money is the primary incentive for refunding, but there are other benefits, such as varied eating and new friendships. Enjoy them all.

Glossary

BLANKS (also called *offer forms, forms*): a form to be turned in for a refund. Available on store pads, in newspaper or magazine ads, and so forth. Blanks may be *refund-offer blanks, cash-plus blanks,* or *sweepstake blanks,* depending on the terms of the offer.

CARDBOARD BACKING: the back of a store pad of forms. Some backings give instructions telling consumers how they may participate in the offer if all the forms are gone.

CASH-OFF COUPONS: discount coupons ($.05, $.07, and so on) given free through public media (such as newspapers and magazines) that you turn in at any grocery store for the specified amount off on the purchase of the designated product.

CLEARINGHOUSE: an outside agency that contracts to handle payment and other details of offers for various sponsors.

COMPLETE DEALS: a ready-to-send-for refund offer, complete with the refund-offer form *and* all correct necessary qualifiers.

CURRENT REFUNDABLE LABELS: the correct qualifier required for an offer that is currently open.

FDA FAIR LABELING REGULATIONS: We interpret Food and Drug Administration (FDA) regulations on promotional offers as governing *only* on-label deals. These may be in the form of cents-off regular price, two-for-the-price-of-one sales, $.01 sales, introductory price specials, premiums attached, or coupon offers. The FDA's definition of coupon is unclear. They may mean an on-label cash-off coupon good toward the next purchase, on-label refund offers, or both. The following are some regulations governing on-label promotions.

Introductory specials can be made only on new or substantially changed products for a period of six months.

Bargain sizes (*economy size, budget pak,* and the like) must be priced at least 5 per cent less than the lowest unit price of other sizes because they lead the consumer to expect a savings.

Cents-off-regular-price labels must represent a true discount over the regular price. A sign giving the regular price must be posted near the stocks of cents-off merchandise.

On-label promotions are limited to no more

than three per year in the same trade area on one size of one commodity. No promotion may last for more than six months, and a thirty-day lapse between promotions is required. Promotions may not exceed 50 per cent of total sales on any one product.

Coupon-promotion details and conditions (such as expiration dates) must be given in a prominent and conspicuous statement on the label and must not be misleading.

Redemption of coupon promotions: "A representation on the label or labeling that the consumer commodity is being offered for retail sale at a reduced price by virtue of a redeemable coupon shall not be used unless the coupon is redeemable at retail unconditionally, or upon the purchase or subsequent purchase of either that product or other consumer commodities involved in the promotion. It is provided, however, that in lieu of unconditional redemption at retail, the sponsor may request that coupons be mailed via first class mail to some central point for redemption only if the consumer is reimbursed for the cost of the first class postage."

An FDA news release stated that "Sponsors of coupon promotions not redeemable at the retail level are required to reimburse the consumers for cost of redeeming their coupon by mail." This ruling, issued in early 1972, was interpreted in dozens of newspaper articles to cover *all* mail-for refund offers; and as many experienced refunders know, there was a great deal of fuss when it seemed that not many companies were repaying refunders for their stamps.

Our advice is to forget it because it does not represent a gain for consumers in the long run. (Companies easily sidestep this by saying that the refund amount "includes postage," that the refund is $.92 plus $.08 postage instead of $1.00, or simply by limiting the number of their promotions to compensate for the extra costs.)

Deeper analysis of this FDA ruling does not indicate that it could govern anything beyond on-label refund offers—and then only if the FDA extends the definition of coupon to cover refund offers.

In fact, the confusion over the definition of the term *coupon* as used by the FDA is the basis of a suit against FDA by the Grocery Manufacturers of America (GMA) and twenty large firms. GMA contends that "Limitations on coupons would substantially reduce legitimate realized savings to consumers, and that FDA's coupon regulations are confusing and unworkable, since they neither define what is specifically meant by 'coupon,' nor distinguish between coupons and other promotions."

Consumers may send suggestions or questions to FDA Office of Consumer Affairs, Room 15B32, 5600 Fishers Lane, Rockville, Maryland 20852.

MONEY-PLUS OFFERS: promotional mail-away-for offers of gifts (merchandise items) given for labels *plus* a money charge, which may be as little as a $.25 handling charge. Most money-plus offers, even those requiring a large amount, represent a substantial saving over the usual retail price of the items.

ON-LABEL DISCOUNT: a statement on the label that the price shown is a certain amount off the regular price.

POINT COUPONS: small-value coupons that are regularly enclosed with, or printed on the labels of, many or all products of an entire brand line.

PROMOTIONAL OFFERS: general term covering any specials, sales gimmicks, discounts, bonuses, refunds, and so forth designed to get consumers to buy a product.

QUALIFIERS: the portion of any label, box top, carton, wrapper, and the like that is required as proof of purchase according to the terms of the offer.

REFUND EXCHANGE: a service to circulate, exchange, trade, or swap various refunding items. An exchange may be a *refund-blank exchange, label exchange, complete-deal exchange,* and so forth, depending on the terms of the exchange advertisement. These advertisements are generally placed in refund bulletins by individual refunders.

REFUND OFFERS: promotional mail-away-for offers of cash, coupons, or gifts given *totally free* for labels, box tops, proofs of purchase (qualifiers).

REQUIRED BLANKS (also called *must blanks*): any form write-up or other blank

GLOSSARY

that states "must accompany" in order for you to qualify for the offer.

SASE: sender is to provide a return self-addressed, stamped envelope. Long (business-size) envelopes are always best.

SHUFFLING FEE (also called *handling fee*): a small service fee that persons exchanging refund offers often charge for their time.

SPONSOR: the manufacturer or company making the promotional offer.

STORE COUPONS: a refund offer in the form of a coupon for a specified amount off on your next purchase of the particular product. It is called a store coupon to distinguish it from cash-off coupons. The discount is generally far greater than it is with cash-off certificates.

SWEEPSTAKES (contests): entries that give you a chance to win a prize. The chance of winning is calculated, by government investigation, to be a million to one.

TRADING STAMPS: a bonus given by the retailer to promote patronage of his store. These are redeemed for merchandise or cash.

USUALLY REFUNDABLE LABELS: labels from brand names that often make refund offers; a portion usually asked for in past offers.

WRITE-UPS: these are the same as blanks, but they do not provide a place for you to write your name and address.